ONLINE CONSUMER PSYCHOLOGY

JOHN LOK

ISBN 979-888606024-9

Contents

Preface

Introduction

I write this book aims to explain whether what marketing ought choose online sale channel, it means that how and why digitial market can let online consumers to reduce to spend more time to seek information in order to achieve any transaction in success in short time.

In part one, chapter one I shall explain how to apply behavioral economic method to predict normal basic income consumption client group's habitual spending behavior as well as how to apply behavioral economic method to predict how labor market changing behavior and predict when labor market changes will occur in order to solve shortage of labor or job supply shortage challenges, I shall explain how can apply behavioral economy method raises basic stable income consumer consumption desire, I shall explain behavioral economy method to explain what is the mean of basic stable income consumption great of small amount desire, how to apply life-cycle advertisement method to predict of consumer behavior, and explain how to apply behavioral economy method to raise electricity consumption from electricity user individual habit.

I shall explain how to apply behavioral economic method to build consumer confidence is as a predictor of consumption spending. I shall also explain what confidence in consumption survey means and I shall apply behavioral economy method to explain how and why to apply survey to gather data in consumption market. It can measure how much degree of confidence of overall clients to the brand of product or service as well as how to build consumer confidence to buy the brand of product or consume the brand of service as well as I shall also explain what a confidence indicator means and how to apply confidence indicator to predict how many potential consumers will choose to buy the brand of product or consume the brand of service. I shall explain how to apply behavioral economy methods to influence employee individual psychology to achieve to raise productivity of long term incentive invention. I shall apply behavioral economy method to explain why increasing salary is short term incentive productivity method, how to improve the design of incentive structures to encourage productivities organizations, how to build employees and managers kindly co-operational relationship method, explain whether bonus method can encourage service performance to be raised as well as how to apply behavioral economy method to explain how to predict human motivation natural behaviors. I shall apply behavioral economic method to explain that why under-level productive efficiency is not represent low production number to the manufacturer as well as low-consumption desire is not represent less consumer demands or customers lose confidence to the product.

In , chapter two, I shall indicate some large organization cases how to apply online channel to achieve sale in success.

In chapter three, explains how and why online sale channel will influence marketing behavior to be improved. I shall indicate some service and product case to explain what the time pressure consumption environment can influence consumer decision making. I also indicate some large international organizations to explain how and why consumers will feel time pressure to influence their consumption behaviors. This second part explains how and why time pressure will influence employees feel that they need learn how to change their working behavior in order to adapt their working pressure environment. In this first part, however, I aim to research whether online marketing time factor can influence the consumer individual consumption desire to be changed either to choose to buy this product or consume this service or choose to buy another product or consume another service to replace the consumer whose original preference choice. If time factor can influence any one consumer individual consumption choice to be changed easily.

Prologue

Table of contents

Long time pressure brings poor performance and customer negative emotion reason

CHAPTER ONE

Stable income consumer individual online time consumption behavior

Economists aim to develop models of human behavior and interactions in consumption markets. But consumers behave in complex ways, such as how to predict consumers to make rational decisions in consumption processes. Moreover, self-consumption control and motivation can vary significantly across different individual consumer.

In order to build useful consumption prediction models, economists make simplifying assumptions, aims to predict how to raise stable basic income consumer target group consumption more success. However, behavioral economy method is one kind of accurate consumption prediction method. It can be applied to predict economic decision-making to every consumer consumption choice more accurate raising whose consumption desire?

I shall indicate how to apply different behavioral economy methods to raise stable basic stable income target consumer group consumption desire in these different consumption situation (consumption environment) aspects as below:

1. Stable basic stable income consumer group consumption great or small amount desire

The consumption of products and services is a fundamental part of consumer's welfare. Basically, every one who has stable basic stable income, who will like to consume any products and services. Even, consumption great or small amount desire won't be depended on whether the person whose income is more or less. It means low income level of people will still like to consume great amount to buy expensive products or consume expensive services, because consumption is human's part of life and basic needs.

This stable basic income people will like to consume, because they have stable income source when they do not worry about unemployment occurrence to cause them have no enough money to support their life. Otherwise, non-stable basic stable income people won't like to consume because they feel they have no stable basic income source to support their life and they will worry about unemployment occurrence any time. Hence, stable basic income people will have more consumption desire to compare non-stable basic stable income people in any countries usually. Behavioral economic method indicates they feel their economic benefits will be loss if they planned to buy any products or consume any services easily. So, they prefer to save money in bank more than consumption.

1. Demand systems and micro-economic factor influence basic income people consumption attitude

Why stable basic income people will like to consume? Because who have more demand, a demand system shows the level of consumer demand for different products and services: e.g. one basic stable income person may refer to the demand for clothes, another the demand for food etc.

How the demand for that particular product varies with the prices and demographic factor will influence who to accept consumption. Such as stable basic income people who will not consider to decide to buy the cloth to wear or the food to eat if who feel the cloth or food price is even more expensive to compare other kind of cloth or food.

Otherwise, non-stable basic income people who will consider to decide to buy the cloth to wear or the food to eat if they feel that they still have enough cloths to wear or enough food to eat at homes , even these food or cloth price are less expensive to compare others. Because they feel they lack stable income effort to support them to consume. Hence, basic stable income factor can influence the consumer's consumption decision.

2. Life-cycle advertisement method can influence consumer individual consumption behaviors to be increased

Consumer behavior makes strong assumptions about the informational and computational bases of consumer behavior. Generally, consumer behavior is reasonably characterized as the maximization of expected lifetime utility subject to budget constraint and conditional on the available information.

Generally, consumers prefer to buy any discounted products or it is reasonable that consumers accept to buy many attractions to persuade them to buy any kinds of bargain discount products. Hence, low bargain discount product is one good behavioral economic principle to encourage or persuade or attract any consumers to increase consumption.

What is behavioral life-cycle model? This model explains consumer behavior can be persuaded to buy any discounted products by advertisement, e.g. television, radio, newspapers, magazine etc. promotion channels. Because frequent advertisement promotion method can let any consumers often remember the product's brand, discounted price, style, color and image from advertisement content.

So, advertisement can be one part of consumer behavioral life-cycle. For example, when the television audiences often watch TV. Hence, when the brand of product advertisement often makes fun image and discounted message to let TV audiences to remember this brand of product, when they are watching TV. Then, it has possible to persuade any potential consumers to choose to buy this brand of any products or consume this brand of any services, due to its advertisement of discounted sale message is very attractive to every one to let this advertisement audience's attention to remember this brand of products or services are selling or serving in market at this moment. So, it is advertisement image behavior influences audiences to buy the brand's any products attractively and persuasively.

3. Raising electricity consumption from electricity user individual habit

For electricity use market case example, how to analyze people's behavior in consuming electricity using a behavioral economic framework ? Electricity consumption is modeled by the means of consumer's individual useful habit, electricity price, consumer satisfaction level, willingness to invest in new technologies, social interactions, and marketing strategies by the power utility. Because electricity is necessary to every home or electric vehicle users needs or businessmen office etc. different needs every day.

Power companies supply electricity to a region's homes and industries. However, electricity needs modernization of power system companies expect to increase price. Due to competitive factor, such as other fuel resource choices, outdated kind of energy electricity supply, and renewable fuel energy source competition.

Hence, applying behavioral economic concept, I assume electricity consumers will compare to electricity and other kinds of energy choices to weigh up the costs and benefits of all alternatives, aiming to maximize their benefits, before making a decision to choose to use electricity for

their house electricity demand or electric vehicle or shop or factory manufacturing etc. function of different aspects of electricity users.
For example, electricity business clients, they aim to reduce cost, such as energy expenditure, when they use any energy to manufacture their products in factories. If they feel electricity is expensive price to compare other kinds of energy power supply. When, they feel that they can not earn much beneficial advantages to use electricity to produce their products. Otherwise, if they feel other any kinds of energy supply can replace electricity to give more benefits to compare electricity energy. Then, many business electricity users will change to use other kinds of energies to consume to replace electricity power.
However, electricity can have competitive ability in electric vehicles market, if many drivers feel environment protection is more important to compare vehicles will be popular to be driven, due to many drivers don't want air pollution. They will like gas vehicles. Hence, the main attribute from the consumer side is one their habit electricity consumption behaviors, satisfaction level, energy efficient interaction with the power utility.
Consequently how to predict electricity consumer's demand. The important factor is how to let electricity users to feel power companies are changing a reasonable level to compare other similar energy supply products. When electricity users feel electricity which can bring more benefits to compare other kinds of energy products. Then, in energy supply market, if the demanding number of electricity consumers can increase more than other kinds of energy demanding number. Then, it is right time to raise electricity price to charge electricity consumers. Hence, how to persuade electricity consumers to feel that they can have more benefits to compare other kinds of energy products. It is the main successful factor to electricity power supply companies.

Consumer confidence is as a predictor of consumption spending

Behavioral economists believe it has link between confidence and economic decisions to cause consumers to choose spending, if the consumer has confidence to believe the product is worth to use, then who will accept to buy the product to use.
Concentrated on the conceptualization of confidence and its role in mode in theories of consumption. It also concerns on whether the confidence indicators contain any information beyond economic fundamentals. The

concern is whether confidence can be explained by current and past value of variables, such as income, unemployment, inflation or consumption or in other way.
Whether confidence measures have any statistical significance in predicting economic outcomes once information from the above variables is used. Economic variable factor will also influence consumer confidence to decide consumption spending, e.g. real consumption expenditures (income, wealth or interest rate).
Finally, it will identify under which circumstances confidence indicates can be a good predictor of household consumption. Hence, survey is one good measurement method to predict whether how much every household has confidence to spend to consume the brand of products to use. Why is survey a good confidence consumption measurement prediction to every household in every country?
The reasons include survey can gather every household consumption habit history data to evaluate whether every survey person has how much confidence to consume the brand of products. Which in most cases correspond to periods where there are large changes in household survey indicators, liking during financial crises or geopolitical tensions to measure or predict whether the country's future good or bad economic condition factor will influence every household consumption desire in the year.
This modelling approach assumes that there is a certain (unknown) in confidence index changes beyond which confidence starts impacting consumption behaviors. So, sample household surveys can show the contribution of confidence in explaining consumption expenditures increases when household survey indicators feature large changes. So that confidence indicators can have some increasing predictive power during the survey investigation period in the year.
Other view point, surveys have been concerned on whether the confidence indicators contain any information beyond economic fundaments. The concern is whether confidence can be explained by current and past values of variables, such as income, unemployment, inflation or consumption or the other way. Whether confidence measures have any statistical significance in predicting economic outcomes once information from different external variable factors to influence the survey household group.

What is confidence in consumption survey ?

Confidence in consumption. For example, to measure whether how much degree of strong inflation in the economy, such as recessions and recoveries will influence the country's household confident consumption in the year. The surveys consumers' questions usually concern on major expenditures and changes in the respondent's financial situation, focus on job availability and current business conditions etc. questions. It is then possible that about consumer confidence depending on the relative performance of the variables that may be more relevant balances, with respect to the factors that determine unemployment and other labor market related issues. It aims to investigate whether those any one of variable factors will influence consumers general loss confident consumption desire in this year.

What is a confidence indicator ?

A confidence indicator is considered as an explanatory variable for consumption together with standard variables used on predicting consumption expenditure. However, the natural real personal consumption expenditure is unexpected and unpredicted easily.

In conclusion, consumption expenditure depends the consumer individual confidence. If the consumer has much confidence to feel this year economic change will be better and he/she is easily to find job, then he/she will accept consumption easily in this year. It seems financial wealth and unemployment etc. economic factors will influence every household consumption desire. So, survey is one kind of good psychological consumption prediction method to predict consumption spending for any country in the year. I recommend manufacturers may choose to apply survey method to attempt to enquire sample survey people to gather data to predict whether what degree of consumption desire to them and find solution methods to solve low degree of consumption desire challenge.

How to apply behavioral economy methods to influence employee individual psychology to achieve raise productivity of long term incentive intention?

Increasing salary is short term incentive productivity method. Behavioral economy assumes labors will choose to do beneficial behaviors to themselves when they feel their work behaviors can earn more benefits to themselves more than their employers in the organizations. Otherwise, if they feel their work behaviors can earn more benefits to their employers more than themselves. Then, they won't choose to do their work behaviors, e.g. raising productivities or work hard. Due to they feel work hard or raise productivities behaviors that only give more benefits to their employers more themselves.

Whether does cheap product price incentive consumption desire to influence effective consumption behavior? Whether is monetary increasing salary payment incentive labors might be willing to work on task? I feel raising labors productivities is similar to raise incentive consumption, which both have similar point, such as increasing salary payment or cheap product price is the main factor to influence incentive consumption or raising productivities. Hence, it seems monetary factor is not the main effort to encourage labors to work hard.

In labor's behavioral economic view point, for example, if an employer pays an employee more doing a task, who might be less willing to work on it, who might be less productive given whose efforts and who may enjoy the task less. If you want your employees to save more for retirement. You may want to give them fewer investment options. If you want them to engage more in a task, you might want offer them an additional alternative, instead of increasing salary to that task. Thus, increasing salary is not only method to encourage productivities of incentives.

How to improve the design of incentive structures to encourage productivities in any organizations?

Any monetary incentive can only encourage productivities in short term. It can not only encourage productivities in long term in any organizations. It is similar to cheap or discount product price can only attractive consumers to buy the product in short term, it can not attract consumers to choose to buy the product in long term, it prefers to have more options to encourage labors to incentive productivities, e.g. investing good beneficial retirement plans. Suggesting that employees do not have free disposal of their investment options. These standard incentives seem irrelevant raising salary monetary factor, they can be quite effective in inducing labors to take particular actions to incentive productivities in long term. Due to when they can hard work, then they have more beneficial retirement plans or investing plans for their retirement. It means when they can achieve the most effective or efficient productivities to the employer for long term. It will give better retirement benefits and investment benefits to the better or even the best performance of employees. Otherwise, the worst performance employees won't earn good retirement benefits and investment benefits, when their employers feel their perform very poor in the organizations in long term.

Hence, increasing salary level method is not one successful long term incentive method to persuade every employee to raise productivities or encourage excellent performance optional method. Increasing salary level is only similar to reduce product price and it is only short term encouragement to consumption or productivities method.

In conclusion, extrinsic monetary factor can not incentive labor's raising productivities more than every employee themselves intrinsic motivation to raise productivities as excellent performance in any organizations. Thus, organizations need to let employees to feel that they can give long term economic benefits to encourage their intrinsic motivation effort to be raised their productivities or performance more effective or efficient in order to achieve long term both win-win economic benefits to employees and employers both.

Building employees and managers kindly co-operational relationship method

If you are an economist, your employer has no without any financial incentive to encourage your economic research tasks in your organization. It is equally difficult to certify that such activity will contribute to your growth of human capital and increased productivity in research or teaching. The standard model, which explains employee's effort only through the way (determined by productivity), is therefore incomplete. In particular, it doesn't consider that incentives to work do not have to be monetary in other words, that there are other things besides the disutility of labor (Kamenica, 2012) and section 1.3 have.

Why will short term wage increasing method only influence short term labor supply to raise productivities? The effect of reference raising wage can be most easily identified on short term labor supply to raise productivities. For US, New York city taxi drivers case, they have to decide every day for low long they are going to offer their services, given the day-to-day variable ability of demand they face (peaking during bad weather and/or when big conferences and public events are taking place in the city).

In the standard model, houses worked should grow with any growth in demand for New York taxi drivers' services. (one day's earning will have only a negligible income effect in the longer run). And yet actual cabbies work less on a demand heavy day. One of possible explanations suggests that New York city taxi drivers expect a certain income, they have set themselves a specific target income, who expect to achieve every day. During low demand for their taxi services, then they work longer hours to reach the target, when during peak demand, their referential income is achieved quickly and they only work short hours. Elasticity of hours worked with respect to their earnings is therefore negative (Lamerer, Babcock, Loewenstein, & Thaler, 1997).

However, taxi driver is either one self employment business or one taxi company employment driving service occupation. It is similar to other kinds of service jobs in societies. Servicing employees, such as waiters, salespeople, securities, customer services, bus drivers etc. different kinds of service occupations. They are not similar to manufacturing occupation to be applied how many amount of piece of products production to evaluate their productivities efforts. Thus these any one of service job nature is depended on their service performance to clients to feel their service performances are excellent to compare general service performance effort of service employees.

Considerably, respectively, I assume that if these service employees‘ managers can build kindly working environment, e.g. manager individual attitude and behavior can let their employees to feel happy to work together in their teams. Then, the managers' kindly as enthusiastic behaviors or attitudes will let every employee more positive encouragement of service attitude to serve their clients in their teams. Then, the client complaining number will be possible reduced, even none of any complains. Hence, building kindly relationship between managers and employees will raise excellent service performance to any organization service nature employees.

Can bonus method encourage service performance to be raised ?

In service job nature of bonus method can also raise employees‘ overall productivities or service performance. For example, when employees got a provisional bonus before the start of the workweek, but were warned that they would lose it on payday, unless they achieve the productivities or excellent service performance norm, they worked more productivities or let many clients to satisfy their service performance. Hence, managers can achieve bonus plan to compensate any excellent productivity or excellent services to them. Then, they can let clients to feel their service performance more satisfactory than employees of a control group who were merely given the standard promise to receive a bonus upon achieving the norm.

The effort was relatively small, however, productivity grew 1%. Interestingly, the effect of a loss was stronger when how teams were rewarded this way, social pressure came to bear on the less productivity team members. When the team members won't earn any bonus. So, long-term productivity gains were achieved through bonuses paid by excellent performance compensation method to compare to low service performance employees receiving no bonuses at all.

Economic views of human motivation nature

There are only two main types of economic actors and by making simplifying assumptions about how these types of actors behave and interact. The two basic sets of actors in this model are firms, which are assumed in this model are firms, which are assumed to maximize their profits from producing and selling products and services, households, which are assumed to maximize their utility (or satisfaction) from consuming products and services.

It seems any employees will choose to do behaviors to achieve to earn much benefits from their organizations. The models of economic behaviors that consider considerate employees' choice of goals, the actions they take to achieve these goals and the limitations and influences that affect their choices and actions.

For university students choose which universities to study case, suppose that any college enrollment students are deciding which courses to study. Thus, it implies that if the university can provide many different kinds of suitable or right courses to any college enrollment students to choose to study. It means that if the university can provide many different kinds of courses to enrollment students to choose to study. Then, it will have much chance to attract enrollment students to choose this university to study. It's competition can be raised by many courses choice factor. but, in fact, it is not absolute right, although the university can provide many courses to provide to enrollment students to choose to study. But, it is not guarantee to represent it must attract many students to enroll this university to study.

For example, suppose that college enrollment students are deciding which courses to choose to study. Although, it has right course to prepare to these enrollment students to choose to study. But, they see a summary of evaluations from hundreds of other students indicating that a certain course is very good in this university. Then, suppose that they match a video interview of just one student to give a negative review of this university of the course. Even when students were told in advance that such a negative review was worse to this university of the course. They tended to be more influenced by the negative review than the summary of hundreds of evaluations, even although such behavior seems irrational. Hence, although many right courses choice has much chance to attract students to enroll this university to study. But, if its bad educational quality from this course from negative review factor, which will influence the enrollment students number to be reduced.

It implies that students will compare this university's the course educational quality whether is better or worse to compare other universities' similar course educational quality, even this university's this course fee whether is reasonable in educational market. This is cost and beneficial comparison behavioral economy principle to all enrollment students before they decide to choose which universities.

Hence, this case implies that universities how to train teachers' teaching skills to let students to feel that they can learn new knowledge from their teaching staffs absolutely. It means how to raise education training skills to raise teachers' teaching performance. It is very important factor to influence the university's teaching development success. So, many courses choice is not important factor to attract many students to enroll the university. Otherwise, although the university can not provide many courses to let students to enroll, but it's teachers can provide excellent teaching service to teach whose students. This is important factor to attract many students to choose to enroll this university to study.

Under-level productive efficiency and low-consumption desire behavioral economic influences

In behavioral economic influence view point, I feel that under-level productive efficiency is the represent low production number to the manufacturer as well as low-consumption desire is not represent less consumers demands or customers lose confidence to the product.

On the one hand, I shall apply behavioral economic method to analyze why under productive efficiency is not represent low production number influence. Otherwise, I feel under-productive efficiency will have possible to increase production number after the manufacturer can review what factor(s) to influence under-productive efficiency.

I shall give reasons to explain as below:

As Jim, P. & Brendan. M. (2013) indicated who had ever been experiencing failure to do their businesses. Although, they had lost a million dollars, but they felt that they can be taught to learn undiscovered knowledge to know how to do their businesses successful by their wrong judgement and decision learning experience. They explained that " in ll risk taking, speculation, business ventures, entrepreneurial activities, it is the loss side on which you must focus first. This is even true for gambling, the gambler determines how much he's willing to bet, and loss, before the game is played. He doesn't wait for the game to end and then let the croupier or dealer assign his wager for him. How do you determine the downside, and how do you control or minimize it? With objective decision making and a plan that has as its starting point the stop-loss parameters"

Hence, it explains any business will have under-level productive efficiencies and low consumption desire business risk. However, to any one entrepreneur, who needs to know it is one game between the himself/ herself and whose clients. They also need to know with objective decision making and a plan that has as its starting point.

Hence, I assume that if the entrepreneur has wrong decision to cause under-level productive efficiency, it is possible that, due to there is no enough employee number to manufacture the product or many employees are not skillful to manufacture all product in normal time or many employees are lazy etc. different factors to cause under-level productivities. However, when they discover their productivities are very low to compare similar competitors their employees' productivities and efficiencies. Then, they can attempt to find what factor(s) to cause low productivities and low efficiencies. it is possible that any one among of these factors case. They include many employees' lazy to influence low productivities or there is no enough employee number or many employees are not skillful to manufacture their products in production process.

Hence, wrong decision or plan is not represent failure. Otherwise, it can give chance to let the entrepreneur to learn whether what the factor(s) is (are) to cause low productivities and low efficiencies in whose product manufacturing process. As I feel that under-level productive efficiency is not represent low production number. Because I assume that if one worker lacks enough skills and manufacturing experiences to manufacture the product, but who can spend less time to manufacture the product and whose spending manufacturing time is same to the another owning enough skillful worker's time to do the product. Hence, I believe that the product quality from the low-skillful worker's manufacturing skill, it's quality will be worse to compare to the product quality from the high skillful worker's manufacturing skill. Hence, if the low skillful worker needs to spend much time to produce the product, but the product quality can be same to the high skillful worker's product quality. It means that it is sure because the low skillful worker has no excellent skill to compare to the high skillful worker to produce the product. Hence, his manufacturing spending time must be longer than the high skillful worker's time. It implies that the low skillful worker spends less time to raises high production number, but his product must be poor quality to sell. Then, his fast and efficient manufacturing speed that is not achieve economic beneficial to the organization's manufacturing process, e.g. less electricity spends to manufacture the product. Otherwise, the low skillful worker's fast and efficient manufacturing speed of behavior will raise the organization's cost in manufacturing process because consumers would not like to choose to buy any low quality product when they can choose which similar products to compare which one has the best quality and cheap price to buy.

Hence, efficient production is not the main factor to influence the business's success. Otherwise, good quality of the product factor is more important to compare it to influence the business's success.

On the other hand, I shall apply behavioral economic theory to analyze why low-consumption desire is not represent consumer demand lose to the business. As Jim. P. & Brendan. M. (2013) also identified " rather than looking for success to follow, who explained the formula for failure to avoid. As an Wang, founder of Wang laboratories said " it is my belief that there are no secret to success." The formula for failure is not lack of knowledge, brains, skills or hard work and it's not lack of luck, it's personalizing losses, especially of preceded by a string of wins or profits. It's refusing to acknowledge and accept the reality of a loss when it starts to occur because to so so would reflect negatively on you."

Thus, as whose feeling to explain why low-consumption desire is not represent less consumers demands or customers lose confidence to the product. The reasons include the causes of low-consumption desire are possible due to worse economic environment factor influences consumption desire to be reduced. It is not due to whether the product price is too high or quality is worse to compare others. Hence, as Jim & Brendan indicated the formula for business failure is not lack of knowledge, brains, skills or hard work and it's not lack of luck. It's not lack of luck. It's personalizing losses, means its reflecting to knowledge and accept the reality of a loss when it starts to occur. As it is applied to explain why low-consumption desire is not represent less consumers demands or customers lose confidence to the product. It's possible that external economic environment changing worse factor to cause the business personalizing losses, it is not reflect who lacks knowledge, skill, hard work factors to cause failure. Hence, ho to predict when and how and why economic environment changes worse will be important factor to predict when and how and why consumption behavioral changes to cause business's success.

Reference

Camerer, C.F. Babrocks, Loewenstein, G., & Thaler, R. (1997). Labor supply of New York city candrivers: One day of a time. The Quacterly Jounrnal of economics, 112 (2), 407-441. doi: 10.1162/003355399555244.

How do you view the outlook for consumer confidence in your key markets next year? Source from : http://www.Just-food.com Confidence survey, Nov.2015

Jim. P. & Brendan. M. (2013) . What I learned losing a million dollars, p.160. Colimbia University, Columbia business school press, New York, US.

Kamenica, E. (2012). Behavioral economics and psychology of incentives. Annual review of economics, 4 (1), 427-452. doi: 10.1146/annurev-economics-080511-110909.

Maselli, 2012 Technology driven job polarization in
EU , 2000-2010. % change in labor supply
skilled/upgrade (ISCED) and labor demand for
skills/tasks (ISOD).

CHAPTER TWO

Online marketing cases

Body Shop case study

1. Apply behavioral economy method critically assess the extent to which whether Body Shop to be a truly marketing oriented organization throughout its 30 years history. Is body shop daily product is one truly marketing oriented organization? I shall apply behavioral economy method to analyze whether consumers will be influenced by economic environment change to influence their consumption desire to choose to buy Body shop products. If consumers won't be influenced to reduce to buy body shop products by economic environment influence, then it will be one truly marketing oriented organization.

● Body Shop Background

The body shop international power line carrier (the body shop) was founded by Dame Anita Roddick in the England in 1976. It sold personal beauty care products, such as baby and child specific products, bath and shower and color cosmetics, deodorants, skin care, hair care, fragrances, sun care etc. skin health products to provide human body benefits. Nowadays, the body shop was skin and body care manufacturer and retailer operating in 55 countries with over 2,100 stores. It had 42 exclusive outlets in Hong Kong. It's missions were to dedicate to pursuit of social and environment change to meaningfully contribute to local, national and international communities in which trade to passionately campaign for the protection of the environment, human and civil rights and against animal testing and to make fun, passion and care part of our daily lives (Adrian, P. 2012).

● What is the difference between production orientation and societal marketing orientation and sales orientation

In behavioral economy analysis, Body shop consumers' consumption behaviors are trend to satisfy needs more than cheap product price. It means that Body shop had built famous brand. It doesn't consider whether its skin health products are cheaper price to compare competitors' price. It needs to concentrate on researching to manufacture many attractive skin health products to let consumers who feel it can give more skin health beneficial advantages to let them to feel why who need to use Body shop any skin health products. Thus, its consumer consumption behaviors are not influence by its price, they are influenced by their skin health function. There are five main marketing orientations of which a company will adopt one. This will determine the way it interacts with the customer. Such as product orientation suggests that a company focuses inwards looking at what it is capable of, rather than the needs and wants of the client; sales orientation is based upon selling existing products with a turnover sale numbers relationship marketing orientation recognizes the value of repeat business over, not only with customers but suppliers as well; societal marketing orientation is relatively new in the scheme of things but suggests on top of meeting the needs and wants of the customer and the organization there is the societies interests to be looked and marketing orientation is based around the needs and wants of a customer to meet business objectives and it assumes that a sale depends on a customer's decision to purchase a product or provide a service.

● What is marketing two levels meaning ?

Marketing can be seen at two levels, the first level is such as a business philosophy, marketing puts customers at the center of an organization's consideration and which is reflected in basic values , such as the requirement to understand and respond to customers' needs and the necessary to search constantly for new market opportunity. In a truly marketing oriented organization, these values are instilled in all employees and should influence their behavior without any need for prompting. The personnel manager would have a selection policy that recruited staff who could fulfil the needs of customers rather than simply minimizing the wage bill in any marketing oriented organization. The other level is techniques of marketing also include pricing, the design of channels of distribution and new product development.

● What are the three components of market orientation ?

The assessing the nature and importance of market orientation for large firms, such as body shop. The three components of market orientation could be analytically separated. The components of market orientation organization include the first component is the customer orientation, it means an organization must have a thorough understanding of its target buyers, so that it can create a product of superior value to give client benefits ; the second component is the competitor orientation, it means any firm should look at how well its competitors are able to satisfy buyers' needs. It should understand the short term strengths and weaknesses and long term capabilities and strategies of current and potential competitors as well as the third component is to develop marketing plans that are not acted upon by people who are capable of delivering promises made to customers and a marketing orientation organization requires that the organization draws upon and integrates its human and physical resources effectively and adapts them to meet client's needs. Otherwise, a production and sales orientation may be appropriate to firms at certain stages in the evolution of markets. Where the dominant business environment is based on the need for good production planning above all, the company that does this best will achieve the greatest overall business success. It is either production orientation, it means organizations that produce what they imagined consumers wanted, rather than what they actually wanted. Planning for full utilization of capital equipment are often seen as more important than ensuring that equipment is used to provide goods and services that people actually wants. Production-oriented firms generally aim for efficiency in production rather than effectiveness in meeting customer's needs . It is either or selling orientation, it means advertising, sales promotion and personal selling techniques are used to emphasize product differentiation and brands and it does not focus on satisfying client needs or desire new product offerings and production led. Hence, one market orientation organization needs to focus on satisfying clients' needs profitably by these marketing mix, such as product, price, place, physical evidence, processed, people and promotion. Anyway ,Market orientation implied that body shop , which ought seek information about clients, such as current and future needs and took action based this information (client orientation); it ought seek information about competitors' current strengths and weaknesses and their long term strategies and took actions based on these information (competitor orientation) ; it ought coordinate the actions taken by sharing clients and competitors information internally (intra-firm communication).

● What is the three components of market orientation ?

The three components of market orientation meant social marketing and understanding boarder concerns and ethical environmental, legal and social context of marketing activities and programs. The cause and effects of marketing clearly beyond the company and the consumer to society as whole. New terms humanistic marketing and ecological marketing were suggested to societal marketing concept.

● What is the social marketing concept ?

The social marketing concept holds that the organization's task is to determine the needs, wants and interests of target markets and to deliver the desired satisfactions more effectively and

efficiently than competitors and the society's welling being, such as body shop had achieved sales and profit gains by adopting and practicing a form of the societal marketing concept called cause related marketing.

● DISCUSSION

Body Shop is marketing orientation organization in 30 years.

Critically assess the extent to which I consider Body Shop to be a truly marketing oriented organization throughout its 30 years history . It seemed body shop had achieved cause-related marketing as an opportunity to enhance their corporate reputation, raised brand awareness, increased customer loyalty and built sales.

It's corporate values were composed of five core values. The first one was to oppose animal testing. The opposing animal testing for both cosmetic products and ingredients began in 1976 years.

In the 1980 year and 1990 year, who successfully campaigned with animal protection groups to change the UK and European laws to support the development products were tried on human

volunteers. Along with the development of technology testing had played a leading role to protect the rights of both human and animals . The second one was to support community trade, it initiated the trade not aid objective of creating trade to help people in the third world utilizing their resources to their own needs. This reflects communities needed a fair price for natural ingredients who purchased from these often marginalized countries. The third one was to activate self esteem. Women were the main customers and employees in the body shop. The fourth one was to defend human rights. The body shop had long campaign on human rights, highlighting abuses and increasing the global awareness of issues by making full use of the geographic advantages of their shops and supporting other human rights organizations. The last one was protect our plant. In 2001 year, huge campaign against global warming was hosted by the body shop and green peace, who advocated the use of recyclable source and materials (Adrian, P. 2012). Although profits were an essential element of long run survival in body shop and it was likely to be overall corporate and marketing objectives, but body shop seemed more to be required level of profits rather than profit that there were many other objectives, which might pursue through its pricing strategies . For example, if body shop wanted to maximize market share or simply survive, a different set of prices would be delivered than if the objectives were to maximize profits. Hence, body shop ought to see viewpoint the marketing side of pricing and it ought not to see viewpoint the production / supply side of pricing if it was a truly marketing oriented organization. The key inputs for body shop to make pricing decision whether it was marketing oriented or productive / supply oriented included production objectives or marketing objectives, demand or supply numbers were considered cost or sale price and competitors or clients consideration factors, such as beauty skin care products in competitive markets demand, i.e. To decide the price whether customers are willing and able to pay is a major consideration in the selection of pricing strategies and levels of demands . Hence, body shop ought to consider demand numbers , it ought not consider production / supply numbers if it was a truly marketing oriented organization. For example, since most of the body shop's factories were still located in the UK, where wages and salaries were much higher than in Asia, so UK itself sale product prices were higher than that from Asia itself sale product prices.

I think Body Shop was a truly marketing oriented organization more than production/supply oriented organization throughout its 30 years history. In fact, Body Shop was experiencing market level growth. It could expand its sales market in Europe, America, Middle East, Asia and Africa etc. different countries. It seemed that it had attempted to carry on marketing research to decide to choose which countries would have more client numbers to demand to buy its personal care products, then it would follow the countries' estimated client numbers to produce its products to sell to the countries. So, it was why some Asia countries sold its bath and shower and skin and hair care and colour cosmetics products more than its fragrances products, such as Hong Kong young people were more acceptable to use bath and show and color cosmetic and skin and hair care products more than fragrances products . It seemed that Hong Kong Body Shop sold fragrance products numbers were less than bath and shower and color cosmetics etc. products. Nowadays, I think the personal beauty care products new businesses which planned to entry this market was more difficult. It was possible than Body Shop was a famous personal beauty care products sale company, it had owned many clients too many years. So , it caused barriers to any new personal beauty care product competitors felt difficult to entry this market .Furthermore, Body Shop had build strong buyer and seller power to increase clients had more confident to use its products, it was possible that who felt its different kind of products could give more health to their skin or body more than other similar personal beauty care products. Moreover, I believe Body Shop had attempted to carry on technological experimenting to aim to build different countries' clients had more confident to use its products forever.

In conclusion, it seemed that Body Shop was truly marketing oriented organization more than productive/ supply oriented organization oriented organization throughout its 30 years history.

2. To what extent are the pursuits of profit and meeting the needs of wider groups of stakeholders incompatible? Whether Body shop pursuits social responsibility aim or profit aim more.

Any companies need to consider the social responsibility during which are the pursuits of profit and meeting the needs of wider group of stakeholders incompatible. Without this self interest, there will be little motivation for firms to provide better services, workers couldn't earn better salaries and clients couldn't aspire for a high level of consumption. Hence, self interest which helps markets work more effectively for the benefits of all. Hence, companies should adopt a code of behavior and conduct and ethical behavior which would not influence any stakeholders groups' benefits to pursuit their profit honestly. Corporate social responsibility is a form of corporate self regulation integrated into a business model. It aims to give responsibility for corporate actions and to encourage a positive impact on the environment and stakeholders including consumers, employees, investors, communities and others and it is titled to aid an organization's mission as well as guide to what the company can give the best benefits to serve its customers. I shall use body shop company as one example to judge whether what extent are the pursuits of profit and meeting the needs of wider groups of stakeholders will be incompatible. Factually, body shop could adopt a code of behavior and conduct and ethical behavior which would not influence any stakeholders groups' benefits to pursuit their profit honestly. Such as, one of the major and most successful initiatives which body shop used an effective supply chain for their products and body shop made use of their sustainable chain supply strategy to ensure that there was the promotion and the maintenance of the social ethical behavior in its business. Hence, it seemed that body shop could be compatible to achieve an effective supply chain to deliver to different countries‘ stores to meet clients who had more need to buy different kinds of skin care products to provide them to choose to buy in the reasonable price choices in the short time. It is therefore in the best practices and interests for body shop to reach out to the communities in their businesses to provide raw materials to help the manufacturers of the beauty products. It also partook in the development of the market for such small scale suppliers. In many cases the body shop tried to outsource its raw materials to its customers. This had ensured the sustainability of its customer base this included it's sensitivity to its environment and the required standards of the labor practices of its partners. Hence, it seemed that body shop could be compatible to help its partners to earn profits and any countries' partners could provide more job chances to unemployed people to work from body shop's outsourcing strategy. Hence, this had been developed by the body shop by including strategies, such as third party logistic providers and intermediaries in which who had no ownership. The body shop was a multinational company also adopted trading to purchasing approach where it shifted from short term where focus of buying articles to long term focus of fewer suppliers. This was an attempt of it to develop quality products where prices were also fair and affordable to sell to different countries‘ clients. It seemed that body shop could be compatible to sell reasonable prices of products to it's clients. Moreover, it had included in its strategies the aspect of business promotion using catalogues. For the same reason, it had been involved in printing of catalogues which were given out to the clients with their purchases. It was important to note that it' catalogues always contained all it's information descriptions and any person who purchased it's products was bound to receive the explanation of all it's product. This was an attempt of it to develop quality products where prices were also fair and affordable to sell to different countries‘ clients. It seemed that body shop could be compatible to provide clear information description in catalogues to let whose clients to know what it's different kinds of style body skin care products ingredients and benefits were , then who could compare it's products to other competitors to decide to buy or not buy fairly.

In Oct. 2007 the campaign for safe cosmetic products, in which 25 multinational companies participated, tested 33 brand name lipsticks and found one-third of the sampled exceeded the limit of lead allowed in confectionery. The affected brands included L'Oreal and Christian Dior. A definite effect would be that consumers would be more concerned regarded the ingredients of products who used, which was likely to have an effect on cosmetics and skin care products were released to capture share. It seemed body shop needed to consider its beauty personal care products were the most ensure to own organic ingredients to let any countries clients (stakeholder) to meet their body health care needs (Adrian, P. 2012).

On the health and natural aspect, body shop had health and safe responsibility to consumers. Although, I felt who had considered this issue because it had 30 years history to operate this business and it had not received any serious negative complaints damage its health product image from clients before. However, with consumers were increasingly informed and were educated, who were now more demanding for more information regarding products and were becoming more aware of health issue. Products with organic ingredients and natural ingredients, such as tea and plants were gaining popular. Furthermore, consumers were looking for healthier substitutes to seemingly unhealthy products, such as color cosmetics. Hence, body shop began to sell the reducing numbers, it was possible due to clients compared it's body care products quality to the other competitors and who felt it's product's ingredients existed some poor ingredients to cause every one's body to be unhealthy. Hence, it's productive processing was very important. It seemed that body shop could be compatible to consider its individual client body skin health issue whether after who had used it's body skin care products to have skin hurt or skin pain feeling. In conclusion, to judge what extent are the pursuits of profit and meeting the needs of wider groups of stakeholders incompatible for any individual business, it is depended on whether the company's any stakeholders, such as employees, clients, suppliers, partners, society (communities) etc. who will have positive or negative influence from it. I feel that it will be incompatible if the company give negative influence to any one of its stakeholder. Hence, if any one company's at least one stakeholder who felt who had negative influence due to it did business to relate to whom unwillingly, then it's pursuit of profits aim would be incompatible to meet it's needs of its any one of stakeholder. Such as body shop will give positive influence to its all stakeholders. Hence, I feel it is compatible extent to pursuit of profit and meeting the needs of its wider groups of stakeholders definitely.

3. What companies, if any have managed to sustainable reconcile these two aims?

I feel that Nestle company has managed to sustainable reconcile to pursuit profits and meeting the needs of its wider groups of stakeholders two aims compatibly. Nestle was the world's largest food and beverage company. Nestle in the United States, which represented seven operating across the USA country and it was the first expanded effort in USA and achievement tied to Nestle 's global sustainability principle and commitment. Nowadays, It served 97% of American householders and Nestle 's mission was to lead the industry in nutrition, health and wellness and to create a more sustainable future. Instead of it's mission was to pursuit of profits aim, it had also achieved specific sustainability commitment and progress in the categories of nutrition, environmental impact and water use, social impact, rural development and responsible sourcing to meet the needs of it's wider of groups of stakeholders‘ aim. On the nutrition, health and wellness aspect, Nestle met the needs to its stakeholder (clients), such as, Nestle rolled out new portion guidance tools and launched an educational campaign and balance your plate to help consumers build nutritious and delicious and convenient meals that met the dietary guidelines for Americans; Nestle also reduced sodium content in many of its most popular brands, such as Stouffer's and DiGiorno and committed to further reduce sodium content by 10 percent in products that did not meet the Nestle; Nestle also reduced sugar content, such as ninety six percent of Nestle 's children's products met the Nestle criteria for low sugar and by the end of 2014 year, 100 percent of children's products would meet these criteria as well as Nestle also removed trans-fat content, such as Nestle committed to reach zero food and beverage products with trans-fat originating to use as functional ingredients by 2016 year. It seemed that Nestle had considered its food and beverage production content whether these content would have negative influence to its stakeholder (clients) nowadays (Adrian, P. 2012). On the environmental impact aspect, Nestle reduced waste during it's food and beverage products were producing. As part of its commitment to eliminate all forms of waste, Nestle reduced 44 percent of waste per ton of product since 2010 year in the USA five factory locations reached zero waste to landfill status by the end of 2013 year; Nestle also considered responsible packaging responsibility, such as

Nestle Waters North America led the USA bottled water industry in light weighting packaging, in part by reducing the plastic content of its 1/2 liter bottles by 60 percent since 1994 year. Since 2003 year alone, more than 3.3 billion pounds of plastic had been saved by Nestle as well as Nestle also adopted responsible sourcing, such as Nestle Purina Pet Care implemented responsible sourcing guidelines for seafood that align with Nestle 's global responsible sourcing guidelines, working with experts to track suppliers and contribute to healthier ecosystem. In 2013 year, Nestle also reached an important target for palm oil, with 100 percent of palm oil now Round table on sustainable palm oil certified. It seemed that Nestle also considerate whether environment would have negative influence occurrence during it's production (Adrian, P. 2012). On social impact aspect, Nestle supported local communities, such as Nestle in USA donated more than $2.3 million dollars to support local United Way organizations; It also provided disaster relief, such as Nestle waters donated more than 685,000 bottled of water and Nestle Purina contributed more than 60,000 pounds of pet food and 41,000 pounds of cat little to local shelters across the USA for disaster relief as well as it grew supplier diversity, such as Nestle works with over 4,100 small, minority, women and veteran owned businesses to help to spur local economies. It seemed that Nestle also considerate social needs. Thus, it is seemed Nestle company have managed to sustainable reconcile these two aims to pursuit profit as well as it also could gave positive influence to its stakeholders. Such as consumer could feel safe to enjoy to eat Nestle company's health foods; societies could be reduced unemployment from its outsourced assistance job to partners; natural environment could be reduced pollution from its productive protection. Hence, it was not actually neglect its shareholders' benefits during it was doing business as the same time (Adrian, P. 2012).

4. What are basic lessons in marketing that the Body Shop might have taken on board in its early years in order to improve its chances of long term success?

The body shop is a global manufacturer and retailer of naturally inspired , ethically produced beauty and cosmetics products. Founded in the UK in 1976 year by Dame Anita Roddick, who now have 2,133 stores in 55 countries with a range of over 1,200 products in Europe, America, Middle East, Asia and Africa. However, the body shop has not entered the China market. It takes a strong position on activism, ethical business, human rights and environmentalism in a global perspective. The body shop is banned in China because cosmetics sold there have to be tested on animals, according to Roddick. In, 2006 when it was bought by the French cosmetics company L'Oreal which is a big player in China. China has launched scientific developing strategy for future the current policies of advocating. Hence, it is the perfect time for the body shop to enter China market. However, prior to that, as an independent member of the L'Oreal family, the body shop has to make decisions on differentiation marketing strategies, market segmentation and marketing position (Adrian, P. 2012). It might have taken two purposes to body shop marketing in its early years in order to improve its chances from short term to long term success. The short term objective was to generate more sales for the body shop. Through, the introduction of a new service, the market up class, it was hoped that clients could try and experience the body shop cosmetic products. Positive experience of using its products could then be developed through their trial using the market up class. It was estimated that this positive experience could push up the sales. The long term objective was to educate the belief of the body shop to the young potential clients, so that who would become those who preferred natural cosmetic products and were loyal to the body shop in the future. Objectives could provide the starting point for marketing plans and strategies and should be specific targets that are obtained but also challenging. Specific, measurable, agreed, realistic and time related objectives might be taken to body shop to improve early years in chances in long term success. It seemed that Hong Kong was one good market for body shop to satisfy an unfulfilled customers needs to pursue body shop investment chance. Therefore, the objective were to push up sales and built a loyal customer basis for the future. For example, Hong Kong was one young student clients growth market to body shop. In the past, one cosmetic products market statistic was indicated that the colour cosmetic retail value had been increasing from 2002 year, HK$938.3 million dollars to 2007 year, HK$1,132,3 million dollars, so percentage was increased to 5.12% . (Adrian, P. 2012). It seemed Hong Kong might be one good skin cosmetic care products developed market to this body shop in early years. The another factor might improve body shop long term success factor was whether body shop had attempted to analyze direct competition. The body shop's direct competition was not from the name brand like Dior, Chanel or Olay, but rather the less well known brands, from Japan or Korea. Along with the great impact of Korean fashion, many Korean cosmetics brands like Missha and the Face shop had already established shops in China. These two brands also promoted their natural ingredients and target the young customer segment as what the body shop products competition concept could be offered to a market to satisfy a want or need and offered five levels, which were the core benefits, basic product, expected product, augmented product and potential product. Each level added more customer value and the five constitute client value hierarchy products of these three brands were all using natural ingredients and simple and natural in packaging. The body shop , however, differentiated itself at the top levels of the five product and transformations the products might undergo in the future.

Marketing management and planning was essential to body shop, it was the implementation of strategies to achieve long run profitability to body shop and growth. When body shop was looking at how it would achieve this in early years in order to improve the chances long term success, its two keys points to consider are: What was body shop man activity at a particular time? And how it would reach its goals? It might design a strategy that insured a consistent approach to offer its skin care products to raise competition in mind the skin care products changing market. These included product line, distribution methods, marketing communication and pricing. For example, achieving marketing research to Hong Kong and China skin care products market to analyze what were these factors to influence these country people who felt needs to buy its skin care products: Such as internal factors include personality, motivation, learning, perception and attitude; external factors included culture, social class, reference groups , family and personal influences and situational factors included time, income, mobility and availability. The reason was because due to consumers bought skin care products to protect whose skin (core benefits) and their expectations if who were willing to pay more basic product. To enhance the product level, body shop skin health product needed emphasize that skin products were natural. Products of the body shop offered the same effective and natural and flavor and unique corporate values. Body shop was mostly natural (augmented level). Far more than the visible products, the shop shop's unique corporate values create the potential value to fulfil customer's desire of making a better health world. It's good corporate desire citizenship went beyond supplying rational and emotional benefits. Body shop might enter China market to improve long term success. The body shop divided its markets to include overseas Pacific Europe, America , Australia and New Zealand, Middle East, Africa and local

UK countries. Adrian, P.(2012) indicated that a sampling questionnaire survey was conducted among 200 consumers, ranging from 18 to 50 ages in May 2006, a total of 170 valid responses that were used for analysis. Among the 170 responses, 66% were females. The findings were:

(1) About 60 % hoped that cosmetics could be a symbol of being environmental friendly.

(2) 90% would choose products made of natural ingredients.

(3) 90% spent less than 300 RMB on cosmetics and skin care products quarterly.

(4) 83% Chinese youth (age range from 18 to 25 ages) were innovators and conscious of environment.

Hence, the body shop might take a share of potential market in China. It should launch its products among younger cosmetic industry were young females who chased beauty and were willing to spend money on it. So, packaging was one of the vital factors in attracting client. The body shop took a unique approach by choosing simple packaging. The package was not made for mature women. It was made for young female students, who could enjoy on international brand at an inexpensive cost. The body shop was not only to meet young people's demand for beauty , but the demand of being responsible to environment and human rights. Hence, the target market of the body shop should focus on young people ageing from 15 ages to 30 ages. Hence, body shop might take marketing research in Hong Kong and China market to have more confident to invest in these market to improve more success. Next, Whether body shop might achieve price strategy to improve to raise success chance. An assumption is when the individual client is considering the price of any a body shop's beauty skin health product. Economic theory suggests that the customer will act in a totally rational economic manner, such that body shop's every client total utility (or satisfaction) is maximized. In deciding whether try or not try body shop's product, which totally rational consumer will carefully equate whether ought to buy or ought not buy body shop's product at the asking price set will maximizing whose utility. In making judgment, the economist assumes that the consumer has perfect information about both the prices and utility of all the other competitive products in the market and that price is the only consideration in choice. Clearly there are unrealistic assumptions. Price could be determined easily when a target market was identified. (Adrian, P. 2012) From survey indicated 64% of the 170 responses spent less than 1000 RMB on cosmetics and skin care every quarter and 24% of their expenditure was between 100 RMB and 300 RMB on cosmetics an skin care. This number could not be ignored if a cosmetics company wanted to enter this large market and be a leader. For the younger generation, the prices of the products could not be high. The price of these main competitors ranges from 10RMB to 200 RMB. The prices in Hong Kong have higher than that in the USA or the UK. And the consumer's purchasing power in mainland China is much lower than that of Hong Kong . Hence, body shop should adopt a price range in China which was similar to that of the USA or the UK rather than of Hong Kong. Once the body shop established greatly reduced and the capability of price adjustment would be achieved accordingly.

Further, body shop might have chain stores selling channel strategy to attempt to achieve long term success. Sample survey revealed that supermarket was for Chinese to purchase skin care and cosmetics. 120 out of the 170 responses hoped that who could choose products from the chain stores in the future, which suggested that the body shop should build up its own stores was regarded as cares about corporate culture and corporate image. It insisted on selling in its own stores rather than setting up counters in a shopping mall. The stores of body shop could be found easily worldwide because of stores were importance in this competitive buyer. Hence, in China, its appearance should be same as worldwide. Some housewives joined the body shop as sales agent and hold sales parties for other housewives. The sales channel allowed the body shop to reach out to more clients by bringing the store directly into client's homes. This would be a totally new method of marketing in China, but it offered a good opportunity for women to choose products and share feedback in a relaxed atmosphere. This fresh concept could attract female consumers. Nowadays, students in China could only obtain famous skin care products and cosmetics brands from campus agents, as who could not afford the products sold over the counters. It was a major problem that agents could not guarantee the ingredients and the quality of the goods. If the body shop could hold small parties to share products and opinions, that would be a good way to boost sales among students. Hence, body shop might take price strategy to Hong Kong and china market to predict whether what price who could accept to raise more confident to invest to this market to improve more success. Further, body shop might also have promotion strategy to attempt to achieve long term success. The body shop adopted environmental friendly manufacturing, opposed abuses of human rights and was accountable for its actions. The unique values attracted numbers of media groups in many countries. This results in its establishing a good reputation without any advertisements. The body shop also joined numerous social causes, which substitute advertisements. In China, however, it was totally different. In this brand new market, most people were out aware of this company. If it carried on a marketing promotion of no commercials it was impossible to reach a high market share. Hence, commercial advertisements were needed in China. The body shop could use this advertisement to give on impression that women should care about their well being both mentally and physically and it had created a sexy grand with simple packaging and without objectifying women. Many brands reach customers directly by colorful commercials and show their products in movies and TV play series. For the sakes of brand image, some movies about human rights , environmental protection and animal protection could be chosen by the body shop as carriers for particular commercial as most of the audiences were well educated, well paid and environmentally concerned. The target consumers of the body shop aged from 20 to 40 ages were energetic , knowledgeable and environmentally concerned. The body shop could give some lectures on makeup or skin care on campuses to raise feeling among students. To reach brand awareness and high brand loyalty , some samples should be given to students by experience marketing approach. Hence, body shop might take promotion to Hong Kong and China schools to let many young people to know why who needed to buy skin care products to protect their body skin to persuade who felt more needs. In conclusion, the body shop was famous for creating a niche market sector for naturally inspired skin care and cosmetic products through it's unique corporate values worldwide. The significance of the body shop's early entry into China market were strongly proposed. Once the body shop decided to enter the China market, the relevant marketing strategies and management should be implemented, such as the market segmentation and market positioning with the proper consideration of Chinese consumers should be studied in order to win the mind share of potential Chinese customers with the right marketing strategies. Overall, the findings of market survey and theoretical analysis strategy support the feasibility of the body shop's early entry into China market.

Consequently, cheap price is not the main successful factor influences Body shop success. The guaranteed skin health critical is the main successful factor to influence Body Shop success. So, Body shop seems a truly marketing oriented organization. Consumers won't be influenced to reduce its products by bad economic change factor.

P&G body and skin product online marketing strategy case study

- How would you explain the success of the fairly brand?
- Can economic changing factor influence consumers choose to buy R&G products?

Behavioral economy analysis, P&G does not need to consider whether its skin and health product price is cheaper than its competitors because it had built confidence to consumers to use its skin health products. Otherwise, it ought consider to manufacture more different skin health products to give its traditional and potential consumers who have more skin health product choices.

P&G fairly brand which mainly sold low value consumer goods, such a household detergents from bar of soap washing products to sell in UK country supermarkets in the beginning. Then, it innovated to produce liquid soap washing products to sell in UK country supermarkets. Further, it continued to innovate to produce soap products, such as the power of four for price of one, launched this low bulk, high concentration soap product to sell more cost effective to sell in supermarkets, even overseas supermarkets. P&G predicted domestic dishwashing machines instead of liquid of soaps , so it innovated to produce dishwasher cleaning fluid detergents products to let housewives to clean their dishwasher after every family used dishwashers to clean their plates to aim to keep their dishwashers to feel more clean to compare to clean by hand washing. Even, P&G will continue to innovate to produce potential anti-bacterial food washes to satisfy consumers' increasing concern over resides on the surface of fruit and vegetables.

In fact, P&G can predict what the new washing products will sell in this washing market, who will be its direct competitors, which are generally similar in form and satisfy customers' needs in a similar way as well as who will be its indirect competitors, which may appear different in form, but satisfy a fundamentally similar need. Such as P&G sold bar soap washing products in the beginning, it aim to satisfy families wash body to feel more clean needs. But, P&G felt it's direct competitors can sell similar bar soap products, so it innovated to produce new liquid soap washing products to raise its washing unique products and was different to its body washing product competitors. On the other hand, P&G also predicted domestic dish washing machines instead of liquid of soaps , so dish washing machines shall be which indirect competitors. Due to housewives can use dish washing machines to wash plates, so who will not use hands to wash plates after eating, it will cause who reduce to use bar or liquid washing soaps to wash their hands. So, P&G innovated to produce dishwasher cleaning fluid detergents products to let housewives to clean their dishwashers after every family used dishwashers to clean their plates to aim to keep their dishwashers to feel more clean to compare to clean by hand washing.

Even, P&G will continue to innovate to produce potential anti-bacterial food washes to satisfy consumers' increasing concern over resides on the surface of fruit and vegetables. Hence, P&G had attempt to raise its competitive ability in fruit and vegetables food and dishwasher machines cleaning market instead of bar and liquid soaps human clean market. It seems P&G threats of new entrants and threats of substitute clean products. In fact, P&G considers it soaps or other washing products whether which will cause chemical harmful to human skin or foods or dish washers after consumers have used its washing products. In the absence of that safety relationship of P&G social responsibility, its brand can act as a substitute in managing buyers' exposure to risk. P&G branding simplifies the decision making process by providing a sense of security and consistency of buyers which may be absent outside of a relationship with a washing product supplier.

P&G brand addresses a number of dimensions of purchase risk which have been identified as: physical(Will it's soap or washing products cause consumer skin harm or foods harm or dish washers harm?); psychological (Will P&G soap products or washing products satisfy consumer's needs for safety of mind?); Performance (Do P&G soap products and washing products work in accordance with consumers' satisfactory requirement?); Financial (Will P&G soap and washing products provide adequate performance with consumers' budget?). Due to consumers will compare P&G soap and washing products to its competitors' risk level to choose which brand washing products can give the minimal risk to harm to their health to decide to buy from supermarkets. Hence, P&G brand needs be built objectively measured (bar or liquid soap products or washing products are such as unique shape and smell and reliability) and the subjective values that can be defined only in the minds of its consumers (such as perceived personality of P&G brand is unique compare to other washing products brands). It means that P&G will be recalled that its brand processes functional and emotional attributes. P&G brand has been variously described as having personality that are ' fun‘, 'reliable ', 'traditional‘ and ' adventurous‘ and it needs to let consumers to feel it can give no harm to whose health after who use P&G soap or washing kind of products. In fact, P&G developed a single strong P&G brand strategy to sell different kinds of washing products, such as bar soaps, liquid soaps, dishwasher cleaning fluid and anti-bacterial food washes etc products, It aims to let consumers who choose to buy to use these kinds of washing products, then who must remember P&G brand. One approach to P&G branding is to apply the same brand name to every washing products which produces. The big advantage of this approach is the economic of scale in promotion. Instead of promoting many minor brands through small campaigns, it can concentrate all of its resources on one campaign for P&G one brand. But, the main disadvantage of this approach is that P&G can pose significant risks of confusing the values of it's brand. If P&G positioned its bar soaps, liquid soaps, dish washing fluid

and anti-bacterial food washes etc. products range as premium priced, top quality, confusion may arise in consumers' minds if it applied the same brand name to a budget version of its washing products. Does P&G brand still stand for top quality? This is a particular problem for P&G new washing product, such as anti-bacterial food washes and dish washer cleaning fluid products which are of unproven reliability. Hence, P&G sells in low price strategy in supermarkets to let many families can buy its different washing products to do trial test whether its innovative washing products which are better quality to compare to other brand washing products to satisfy who to choose to buy P&G brand washing products for every families to use long term.

In fact, UK soaps product is a imperfect competitive market. The different soap manufacturing companies produce similar color and shape bar or liquid soap products and they build different brands and they are targeted at specific segments, such as family group and they need promotion to promote their brands and soaps price is premium sustained. Hence, P&G needs a differentiated product may have significant monopoly power in that it is unique, but if it fails to satisfy customers‘ needs, its uniqueness has no commercial value. However, P&G had innovated it different bar soap products to liquid soap products, even it also launched dishwasher cleaning fluid detergents products, due to dish washer machines reduce housewives to use hands to wash plates to use soap to clean whose hands after eating as well as it launches potential anti-bacterial food washes to satisfy consumers' increasing concern over resides on the surface of fruit and vegetables. Hence, P&G aims to be any new cleaning products leader to raise its cleaning market share effort.

The soap and other detergents manufacturing industry of Procter & Gamble (P&G) trends and characteristics who its primary intended is target client group(s). I think families (householders) or student individual daily consumption are P&G main target client groups. Soaps are personal care products. Consumers will compare different brands of soaps to decide which brand soaps ingredients can give health to them to wash their bodies and skins. The soap industry includes (P&G) and other soap manufacturing companies primarily engaged in making soap, synthetic organic detergents, inorganic detergents and crude vegetable and animal fats. In general, skin care soap sales include bar soap, body wash and liquid categories which can sell in supermarkets and discounting retailers and drug stores. Traditional , bar soaps, which are considered a mature category, exhibit very low growth, when newer products (shower gels and body washed) substitute products are launched. However, natural soaps still have opportunities for growth if which can be launched to raise care to skins and bodies health to human. The soap and personal products industry is being driven to a large extent by the changing age composition of the population, specifically, baby boomers have established anti-aging preparation as the chief benefit of health products aimed at correcting or improving the physiological condition of the skin. They have led the broad personal care sector of the economy to focus on the potential in aging consumers. Growth is occurring in a variety of age-sensitive product markets from soaps and skin creams to massagers and body fat analysis machines. As baby boomers lives get busier, stress relief soap products will become more important to carry on launching their skin care health quality for human benefits in daily washing. The group composed of 45 ages old to 54 ages old females is responsible for the highest amount of sales of body care and bath products in mass stores, who can influence householder families members spending effort in soaps consumption. P&G soaps are displayed to supermarkets to retail, the supermarkets' shelves are remained unaffected by the changing population in the personal care products sale areas. Even retailers like Brook stone and Sharper Image expanded their interest in branded personal care items. Not only was more retail dedicated to the personal care products, but they were often placed in specific "spa shops" within the store, with displays used extensively to merchandise the personal care category. Body boomers are not, however, the only group important to the growth of this personal care industry. The number of personal care products designed specifically for children is increasing. Health and beauty aids suppliers are using licensing to tap into the growing spending power of children. The traditional soaps manufacturers must carefully review their marketing and other business strategies in order to adapt to the transformed market. The changes also create better opportunities for new personal care product companies to enter particular market segments. The mass bath and body care category has made recent introductions reflective of several trends that department stores, salons and special boutiques have been offering for years. The world consumers are changing their personal care demand to cause a result of soap product innovation, so P&G also needs to replace older well known soap products with newer ones that contain special formulations. New product activity and the increasing popularity and liquid soap increase competition in this personal care market. A growing perception among consumers that who must deal with problem skin and rising levels of concern about germs are helping drive sales of personal soap. Although, traditional brands such as Dove, Dial and Irish Spring still hold the largest portion of the toilet soap market smaller special soap manufacturers are increasing their market shares. Hence, P&G needs to focus on concentrating who its specialty soaps. In general, consumers want a soap that fits their particular needs and specialty soaps, often made with natural ingredients to protect bath and hand skin health. However, some competitors choose to sell soap substitute products, such as oils, bath blends, perfumes and fragrances in supermarket. Hence, these personal care products can also influence P&G company liquid soap sales in overall soap retail market. In soap manufacturer industry, the naturals trends is also evident in the ethic segment of skin care. Ethic consumers are seeking multi-functional products full of botanicals and vitamins butter natural ingredients. So, I think P&G needs to launch this kinds of new class of skin care product to raise its skin class of skin care product to raise its skin care health care to increase consumers' confidence. Due to personal care products market competition is increasing, such as one stop shopping stores can offer for a variety of health related items, healthy foods, dietary supplements, prescription and over the counter drugs, skin care products and other natural personal care products. In addition, smaller natural skin care manufacturers are staying competitive by targeting skin-related over the counter drug markets. Moreover, internet retailing of personal care products has grown rapidly. Web site can offer can be nearly limitless. One important advantage held by online sellers over stores with physical locations is the constraint caused by a lack of shelf space. The characteristics of online sellers allow them to stock a much wider variety of the products consumers want, if also provides an opportunity for small or large manufacturers audience of consumers. One of the greatest difficulties faced by a firm wishing to enter a consumer products market is persuading retailers that they will benefit by dedicating scare shelf space to the manufacturer's products to online selling reduces that problem.

A potentially important negative aspect of electronic commerce for personal products is that inability to feel and especially, smell the merchandise. Many personal care products list fragrance as an important characteristics. To the extent consumers are already familiar with a special products, this is not a problem, but such as P&G getting a new liquid soap products might be more difficult. Soap industry needs to launch to improve soap qualify to satisfy consumer need. It must need enough workers to help P&G to manufacture enough different kinds of soap to sell to different countries soap market. I think its workers include these kinds , such as packaging and filling machine operators, first line production supervisors, cleaning, picking equipment operators, hand packers and packagers, hand material movers and soap researchers because it needs these workers to help it to produce different kinds soaps in the manufacturing process in factory, so it needs to give training to raise whose proficient skills to prepare to produce any new kinds of soap efficiently and it needs to consider the labor supply to soap manufacturing market , e.g. who needs to know what the difference between chemicals and all natural ingredients to prepare to produce its soaps ethically. Because if they have errors in the manufacturing process to cause consumers feel to use P&G soaps to have chemical negative health response. These workers shall influence P&G health soap products image negatively. Hence, P&G needs to consider its workers' working attitude ethically. However, P&G was the largest soap maker and it did not own the most part maintain in house chemical manufacturing capabilities. P&G must therefore purchase new materials from other suppliers, so P&G needs to consider its raw materials suppliers market to measure whether who can give it the largest benefits and the cheapest costs both, Thus, giving the raw material suppliers global marker to choose who remain a greater incentive to provide superior service to P&G. I think P&G needs to spend time to choose who is its raw material suppliers who can provide the best natural health quality and the least chemical ingredients to cause consumers to use to feel uncomfortable response to their skins negative influence. Hence, I think P&G ought innovate its soap products quality to satisfy to avoid to use any cheap chemicals ingredients to produce its old or new kinds of soap products to sell to consumers unethically if it still wants to a sale leader in this personal care product market.

2. How do you think Procter & Gamble has been able to increase its market share at a time when competition from supermarkets' own-label brands has intensified?

Procter & Gamble operates mainly low value consume products, such as household detergents are among the most competitive and building successful brand is key to long term profitability. Differentiating one product from another in the minds

of consumers can be extremely difficult, with one packet of detergent looking very much like another and performing similarly. It seems that it can not be unique to sell in supermarket. However, then it innovated new liquid soap products, it seemed to adopt to change in consumer preference, and maintaining consistent standards when exploiting new market opportunities. Adrian, P. 2012) showed that Fairy liquid was rated as Britain's number one cleaning brand by Marketing magazine and in 2010 accounted for 3 percent share of the UK washing up liquid category by value. The brand has been a regular household feature since the name first appeared in 1898 year on a bar of soap. P&G first launched Fairy liquid in the UK market I think Procter & Gamble (P&G) has this marketing strategy to supply its soap products to supermarket retailers. A supermarket is not only supply to likely to encounter a massive range of products, such as food , drink, homecare, personal care, luxury products etc. Consumers can see categories and see how much the offering changes, the range , the packaging , the branding and advertising or promotion of any brand products sale at shelves. Hence, such as P&G manufacturer in 1960 year. At the same time, the market for washing up products was still in its infancy, with most consumers using solid soaps, and only 17 per cent of households using liquid soap. But P&G gained most from a change in consumers' habits. It educated the public of the benefits of using washing up liquid. The launch of Fairy liquid soap products involved distributing 15 million trial bottles to about 85 per cent of household in the UK. Creating early awareness and trial of the Fairy liquid soap innovative products led to Fairy gaining a market share of 27 per cent by 1969 year. It had a proud positioning as a slightly more expensive product which is better value and worth. So, it created brand values of a soft, caring, homely image by advertisement promotion. It also attempted to adopt in response to changing attitudes, for example, a commercial in 1994 year for the first time used a father instead of a mother at the kitchen sink. During the first twenty years of the brand's life, product innovation had been relatively modest. However, an increasing competitive market, customers have forced P&G to innovate in order to maintain and strength its market share.

Adrian, P.(2012) showed that with emergence of many 'me-too' competitors from supermarkets, Fairy needed to offer additional unique advantages to raise its competition. In 1984 to 1985 years, P&G introduced a lemon variant of Fairy and its total market share increased to 32 per cent. By 1987 year the market share had increased to 34 per cent, with the newly introduced lemon variant accounting for one-third of sales. In 1988 year, a new formulation was launched , offering 15 per cent extra mileage, as well as more effective grease eradication. In 1992 year, the original Fairy Liquid was replaced with Fairy Excel, which claimed to be 50 per cent better at dealing with grease. This helped to increase the market share to 50 per cent . In the following year a concentrated version of Fairy Excel Plus was launched, with the slogan ' The power of four for the price of one'. P&G launched this low bulk, high concentration product to retailers, such as supermarkets, who were tiring of filling their valuable shelf space with more and more variants of basically low value products. Excel Plus offered supermarkets more cost effective and profitable use of their shelf space. Increasing ownership of domestic dish washing machines posed a threat and also an opportunity to Fairy. The threat came from a relative decline in sales of liquids used for hand washing of dished. The opportunity arose from increased demand for dishwasher cleaning fluid and the Fairy brand was extended to dishwashing detergents. In 2006 year, P&G introduced Fairy Active Bursts for dishwasher. Excel Plus was launched in the UK, Denmark, Finland, Germany, Holland, Ireland and Sweden etc western countries' supermarkets to help it to sell.

Innovation and reliability have been at the heart of Fairy's branding strategy, in a market which has been contested by other manufacturers' brands, and increasingly by supermarkets' own label brands. Preferences for new scents of detergent are continually emerging and provide an opportunity for innovation. Following a series of food safety scares, some observers of the market have pointed to a potential market for anti-bacterial food washes which would satisfy consumers' increasing concern over resides on the surface of fruit and vegetable.

Its innovative liquid soap products, it needs supermarkets where which compete with other soap product manufacturers for the attention and hopefully the purchases to shoppers choice. It's a soap products from bar soap to liquid soap kind of products. P&G brand have been a player in the household and consumer personal care products market for nearly 200 years. They started life making candles at a time when there were still a common source of domestic lightly. But they moved on from those to other related products, soaps and cleaning products. Today, P&G have around 300 brands, including Crest Oral Care brand, Pampers Nappies brand and Baby products, Tide and Arial brand washing powders, Tampax Sanitary products etc. different brand in this personal care market. To keep a range as wide as this refreshed and to develop new and improved produce to feature on the supermarket stages around the world needs a powerful innovation engine. P&G had built a world wide research and development operation which involves some 7500 scientists and a spent of around USA$3 billion per year. It might be not as much as the high technology pharmaceutical industry, but still very impressive for its sector. P&G had some very effective systems and structures to ensure efficient soap products innovation project selection and progression . P&G had an impressive record on new product launches and many of their new categories billion dollars brands, products magic whose annual sales could be high as US$150 to US$200 million. But, in the late 1990 year, there were concerns about this approach to innovation. When if worked there were worries, not least the rapidly rising costs of carrying out research and development cost. However, I think P&G should not raise its new kinds of soap products sale price, such as liquid soap products. Even it had spent too much research and cost development expenditure. Hence, I think it still needs to keep competition to attract different countries consumers to buy from different countries consumers to buy from different countries supermarkets globally. Hence, low sale price is its major market strategy in supermarkets sale make. For long term, I suggest P&G chooses to outsource its research and development internal business department to one or more than more external technological research and development consultant company/companies to carry on researching any new soap products to avoid spending too much expenditure to raise soap products sale prices to reduce its competition to sell in supermarkets. P&G 's pioneering use of advertising, direct distribution , marketing research , brand management and produce innovation strategies to raise it's growth throughout the 20th century. Diversification, globalization of it's brands, innovations in distribution and supply chain management and P&G 's technological and product innovation strategy continues to drive its success into the 21st century. P&G had pioneered a series of strategic innovations had sustained its competitive advantage in a number of highly competitive market and its primary focus was process innovations in many areas.

Firstly, background on P&G was from its origin to 2008 year briefly reviewed. Next five strategic innovations were each reviewed along with its competitive implications in the areas of direct to consumer advertising, direct product distribution, marketing research, brand management and technological and product innovation. Hence, P&G soap products innovation was divided to two stages of two different periods to aim to satisfy consumers' body and skin health needs of bar soaps choice to use liquid soaps choice in this personal bath and washing care market.

Adrian, P. (2012) showed that in 1915 year, P&G opened a facility in Canada representing its international operations. A chemical division was created during 1917 year and 1918 year which was responsible for research and development of new products. To sell these new products. P&G created a market department in 1924 year. The purpose of this department was to study consumer preference and purchasing inhabits (Data monitor, 2008:7). In 1926 year, a perfumed bar of soap was introduced. By the end of the 1920 year P&G had no longer produced candles, thereby signal a major shift in its core business . Then, 1933 year, the acquisition lead P&G into hair care products. In the early 1940 year, P&G established a drug products division which also developed and sold a variety of toiletry items.Then, P&G introduced new products and entering new markets, it had not stopped innovating on its established products , such as tide liquid soaps was launched in 1984 year. During this time P&G also purchased Blendax a popular tooth paste brand in Europe. As the 1980 year, P&G made a significant move in Asia by entering into a joint venture to produce products in China. In 2007 year, it invested US$35 to US$50 million in its Gillette manufacturing facilities in South Boston, USA. At the same time, it announced a restructuring whereby P&G. Beauty and health division would be managed under the P&G purchased HDS cosmetics laboratory skincare line that focuses on specific skin conditions that require more attention than general cosmetics. P&G 's history of marketing innovation began in 1980 year with Ivory soap on what had been promoted around the world as the floating soap (Dyer et al., 2004). Ivory represented P&G 's first attempt to brand a product through the use of advertising to connect with customers. Direct to consumer advertising was an innovation P&G pioneered with its customers and as such was a major innovation versus the traditional practice of advertising to wholesalers and practice of advertising to wholesalers and other distributors. During the 1800 year's soap was cut from huge soap slabs at the local grocer. Soap was a classic commodity with each manufacturer's product virtually indistinguishable from others. It is believed that P&G 's technological innovation was making Ivory out of Palm and Coconut oils, both less expensive than olive oil that was the basis of better soaps of the soaps to be mass produced and felt of finer higher quality soap (Dyer et al., 2004).Unlike other soaps of that, Ivory ingredient was lathered, easily and floated in water without melting. The unique blend of the soap meant that P&G could sell the soap in a premium market, such as supermarkets. However, since it used less expensive inputs, this led to higher margins. Those higher margins provided the mass to pay for advertising to raise the profile of the soap (Dyer et. al., 2004), thereby creating the brand and the beginning of a product differentiation strategy to sell in supermarkets.

3. To what extent can the principles and practices of brand management used for fairy liquid be applied to other goods and services, such as televisions and package holidays?

I think the brand management principle used for P&G brand, fairy liquid soap products sale which is more similar to apply to any television brands management products sale. Otherwise, the brand management principle uses for P&G brand, which is not more similar to apply to any package holidays travel services. Firstly, televisions and liquid soaps which have similar characteristics, such as they are products and it can be touched, seeing it existence and they are needed to launch to adopt consumers' taste, e.g. consumers link to accept to use liquid soaps more than bar soaps popularly as well as consumers like to watch colorful and clear image of televisions more than black and white image of televisions. Hence, any soaps and televisions companies which need to launch high technological televisions or more health ingredients of soaps to satisfy consumes' needs seriously if which wanted to build their brands famously and which wanted to retain old consumers and attract more consumers to buy their products in this skin care and television entertainment markets. Otherwise, if some companies did not continue to launch their television or soap products. I believe these companies brands will be not popular, even consumers will forget their brands existence due to other companies continue to launch their televisions or soaps to build strong brands in those skin care and television entertainment both product markets competitively.

Anyway, any one travel agent's package holidays travelling service is not similar to P&G brand fairy liquid soap products characteristics. Due to package holidays travelling services which can't be touched and can't be seen, the package holiday visitors who can only feel the travel agency whether whose travel journey itinerary arrangement, e.g. travelling destination, travelling date and time, travelling living apartments, hotels, restaurants, leisure activities, air tickets prices, airlines choice etc. whether this package holidays travelling is suitable to him/her only or whose family or whose friends with her/him together. The most importance, package holidays travel services are not similar to soap or television products which need to often launch whose skin care and seeing entertainment products to adopt consumers' needs. Although, the travel agencies sometimes need to reorganize new travel journal itinerary , e.g. seeking England, United States fresh and unique travelling places or cheap hotels who travelers choose popularly. But, travelling industry is seasonal period leisure business, it means that public holidays will have many consumers. Hence, basically, the seasonal periods are limited to travel agencies to build whose brand easily. It means that the client numbers are influenced by the seasonal periods, their numbers will not have much changing, even the travel agent often spend much effort and time to seek any new and unique travel journey itinerary holidays package. Although, travel agencies do not need to spend much money to invest to launch its package holidays travel arrangement service. But, they are existence in one competitive travel market. Every travel agent package holidays travel service price is controlled by the seasonal period whether the period is holiday or is not holiday and what the travelers' feeling to the country, e.g. safety extent, shopping places and prices extent, air ticket prices extent, accommodations and restaurants prices extent. These factors are controlled by the travelling countries. Agencies are difficult to differ their packages holiday travelling services to win other travelling agent competitors to build strong brand management famously. Due to which cannot control external factors to influence their price competition easily, such as airline companies air tickets prices, the destination (country) which hotels, restaurants, leisure services and transportation prices which are controlled by the travelling destination country's businessmen directly. It implies any travel agencies are difficult to build unique strong brands to attract many travelers who choose to find which to help them to arrange packages holiday travelling services to earn more commissions easily. However, if the travel agency had owned only concentrated on arranging packages holiday travelling services experiences and it had many prior packages holiday travelling consumers who feel that it can arrange the most suitable packages holiday travel arrangement services to let them to satisfy all different packages holiday services. I believe who will only choose this travel agent to help them to arrange any packages holiday travel arrangement services again, even who will introduce its packages holiday travel arrangement services to their friends to know the travel agency's brand by mouth speaking individually. It seems that a new or an old travel packages holiday travel arrangement services agent who ought need more old customers who can speak to whose friends to know how it can give excellent travel packages holiday travel arrangement to them individually, so television or radio or newspapers media travelling advertisement channels do not need promote long time if whose old consumers feel which can provide excellent packages holiday travel arrangement services to make them to enjoy satisfactorily. Hence, it's old consumers' feeling whether who satisfy or who do not satisfy its packages holiday travel arrangement service which will influence the travel agent to build its brand successfully in this packages holiday travel arrangement market. Otherwise, a new or an old television products brand sale company needs more magazines, radios, televisions advertisement to promote which television products for long time due to every family who have different demand to choose to buy the television products, e.g. size, design, manufacturing history and manufacturing country's price. It implies the family can't influence to whose friends to decide to buy or not buy the television brand easily. Due to every family has different demand to choose which kinds of television company brand. The television brand's any different style of television products of the family to choose is not same to or influence to whose friends television brands, so the television brand's buyers speaking will not influence whose friends whether to choose or not choose to buy the television brand easily. Furthermore it will take a closer look at the motivational world of the travel agency staff and how both groups interact. These questions will be analyzed with regard to its significance and applicability in brand management. The results of a neuropsychological systems of package tourists and travel agents with a psychological test.

When investigating the travel market it must be taken into consideration that it is subject to considerable changes due to , for example new dynamic production processes, price comparing systems, the growth of online providers etc. Every travel agent needs to make each brand unique and distinguishable in its perception . The key issues discussed where: Why do package tourists buy? Which scopes and potentials are there ? When positioning style brands? How can potential customers be better addressed and won as a customer? Central question concerning travel agents where: What is there main motivation (commissions, incentives) ? How can travel agents be addressed more effectively? How can travel agents help to increase the sale? Sensing versus intuition concerns perception itself, thinking versus feeling are decision strategies based on perception and judging versus perceiving relate to the handling of these decision . Because individual travel agent needs explain why their choice of packages holiday arrangement is the best suitable to every consumer considerately when the consumer is the first time to contact the travel agent , so the travel consultants need have professional image to make whose visitors to believe whose packages holiday arrangement is the most right to satisfy them to travel in their journeys. Otherwise, one of television brand seller who does not need to build more professional image, due to who is only the television company brand representative, whose duties are needed to explain what the television features and functions to let whose customers to compare to other brand television products when who enquires any one of television brand seller. However, travel agent must need to seek any packages holiday travel informational to let any consumers to choose to let them to compare whether which packages holiday arrangement service is the most suitable to who from the travel agent immediately. Hence, a package holiday travel agent seems to be a travel economist, who needs to compare which packages holiday arrangement is the most right and the most reasonable price to follow travel data gathering to adopt to every customer needs after whose customer spends whose packages holiday arrangement to feel satisfactorily if who want to help whose travel company to build famous brand of providing excellent packages holiday arrangement successfully in this travel market. Hence, any packages holiday businesses which travel consultants seem to be individual mouth speaking advertising to every visitor when who enquire whose packages holiday arrangement ideas to achieve aim to let every visitor to feel travel consultant can suggest the useful packages holiday arrangement because who must not have confident to arrange their travel plan by himself or herself. It seems that a new or an old travel packages holiday arrangement service agent which needs more old customers who speak to whose friends to recognize its existence to build its brand for long term. So television or radio or newspapers travelling advertisement do not need to spend long term if whose old customers feel which can provide an excellent packages holiday arrangement service to them to enjoy satisfactorily. Hence, its old consumers' feeling whether who satisfy or who do not satisfy its packages holiday arrangement service from the first time, they shall influence whose friends or relatives who decide to attempt to enquire the travel agent successfully. Otherwise, any one of television brand sale persons who do not need to build more professional image, due to the sale persons are only the television company brand sale representative, whose duties only need to explain what the television features and functions to let the customers to compare to compare to other brand television products to decide whether who ought to buy the brand television or ought not to buy the brand television. However, any travel agents must need to seek any packages holiday information about airline air tickets prices, itinerary journey and hotels, transportation, restaurant meals, leisure activities of the travel destination country to let any consumers to choose the different packages holiday arrangement programs to compare whether which packages holiday arrangement program is the most suitable to their travel needs immediately. So, their satisfactory extent to the packages holiday arrangement from the travel agent's consultant who can influence their friends or/and relatives to feel whether the travel agent can help them to arrange packages holiday satisfactory. Otherwise, a new or an old television product brand company needs more advertising from magazines, radios, televisions to promote which television products for long term, due to every family who have different demand to choose to buy the television products, e.g. television size, design, manufacturing history and manufacturing country and prices etc factors which can influence every family choice. It implies the family can't influence to whose friends or/and relatives to decide to buy or not buy the television brand easily. Due to every family members who have different demand to choose which kinds of television company brand. Furthermore, it will take a closer look at the motivational world of the travel agency staff and how both groups interact. These questions will be analyses with regard to its significance and applicability in brand management. The results of a neuropsychological study, which measured the implicit personality systems of package tourists and travel agents with a psychological test. When investigating the travel market , it must be taken into consideration that it is subject to considerable changes, due to , for example, new dynamic production processes , price comparison systems, the growth of online providers etc. Every travel agent needs to make each brand unique and distinguishable in its perception. The key issues discussed where: Why do package tourists buy? Which scopes and potentials are there? When positioning style brands? How can potential customers be better addressed and won as a customer? Central question concerning travel agents where: what is there main motivation (commissions, incentives)? How can travel agents be more effectively? How can travel agents help to increase the sale? Sensing versus intuition concerns perception itself, thinking versus feeling are decision strategies based on perception and judging versus perceiving relate to the handling of these decision. Because individual travel agent needs to explain why whose choice of packages holiday arrangement is the best suitable to every consumer considerably when the customer is the first time to contact the travel agent , so travel agent is needed more professional travel knowledge to arrange the best packages holiday to serve every visitor to enjoy their holidays satisfactory to build their brand. Otherwise, any television brand company sale representatives who only need to introduce what the style of television product which feature to let the visitor to know to decide to buy or not buy it. So, any television product brands which need more different kinds of advertising to help them to promote to build their brands long term.

In conclusion, P&G fairy liquid soap brand management principle, which is more similar to apply to television product brand management principle, which need to launch their different style products to satisfy clients needs. Such as P&G brand company needs to continue to change its product ingredient to let many customers to feel to use safely , e.g. it launches bar soap products to liquid soap products as well as any television product companies to launch how to change television images and colours to be more clear to attract many customers to choose to buy whose television brands products. Otherwise, packages of holiday arrangement tourism service, tourism consultants need to own professional travel knowledge to help whose visitors to arrange any the most reasonable price and the most safe and the most unique journeys to attract any visitors to choose whose packages of holiday services. In fact, travel agents who do not need to spend much money to invest to carry on launching their travel service to raise time to gather travel information to increase whose ideas to achieve to persuade every visitors to choose packages of holiday arrangement successfully. Hence, it seems P&G fairy liquid soap product brand management principle which can not apply to packages of holidays travel arrangement service clearly and it's expensive price and many similar products competitors factors which can influence consumers to choose to buy its products. So, in behavioral economy analysis, consumers are influenced to choose to buy its products by economic variable influence.

Mobile phone company online marketing strategy case study

1. Critically evaluate methods that mobile phone companies could use to assess buyer's likely response to new features, such as video on demand and whether its sale number is not influenced by economic environment changing influence?

Behavioral economy analysis, it indicates mobile companies need have internet, video function, GPS location search etc. different high technological functions to attract mobile consumers to choose to buy their mobile products. Thus, if the mobile product can have unique high technological functions to satisfy mobile consumers' undiscovered useful needs. Then it charges higher price and it won't decrease mobile customer number.

Mobile phone is a product to satisfy customers' verbal communication needs during who leave home to need to communicate with anyone urgently . Mobile products are only bought for the verbal communication benefit. In other words, a mobile phone product is of value to someone only as long as it is perceived as satisfying some extra need, instead of verbal communication, such as watching video demand from internet when people are sitting on buses, or trains , or drive cars to watch video entertainment from their mobile phones. So, a mobile phone can be a material product, it can also provide an intangible service, such as verbal communication and watching video or sending email from internet by an 3G or 4G telecommunication fast speed internet service provision channel when who leave their home, who can also enjoy to watch video and call anyone and send email such as staying at home. However, mobile phone is a high level of emotional involvement communication product by the buyer due to there are many different and similar style of mobiles to provide to customers to choose to buy, so I think the mobile phone can provide watching video from internet feature is prefer to buyer to choose more than the mobile phone can not provide watching video from internet , even it's price is more than the non video watching mobile due to young people like to watch video instead of going to cinemas to see movies, it is possible who have no time or who feel movie tickets prices are expensive. Mobile phone is low level of accessible product, due to buyers can use home telephone when who stay at home or who can use any restaurant phone if who is walking on the street , it's location is near to restaurants. Mobile phones are shopping goods, due to consumers generally put a lot more effort into choosing shopping different style of mobiles to buy. Their evaluation include price, credit facilities, guarantees, after sale service, email or video entertainment from internet service. Different brands of mobile products are distributed through fewer retail outlets and therefore there is likely to be a higher margin for the retailer. Customers are usually willing to travel to an outlet to find a brand style of mobile, rather than expecting it to be available on their doorstep. Large amounts of money may be spent on advertising to develop strong brands, such as 3G and 4G telecommunication provision service to watching video or sending email from mobile internet. In fact, mobile product needs to provide intangible service, such as verbal communication , watching video, sending email. Hence, many mobile users ought prefer to buy the brand of mobile company which can provide these kinds of services because who feel these services are whose basic needs, specially the students like to use mobiles to watch video entertainment or working people like to use mobiles to send email to their offices to keep communication when who need to leave offices to work outdoor. However, watching video on mobiles is one new idea to focus of whether who need this service, it can be unclear who the customer is and it can be difficult to conceptualize the exchange that takes place between the provision video watching service of mobile buyer and the mobile seller of the idea. Hence, mobile phone companies need to do market research to evaluate who are the preferable ages segment group and what factors which will cause who do not choose to buy their mobile brands of watching video mobile products. Mobile phone industry is a product innovation industry. Nowadays, mobile phones have these features, such as cameras, MP3 players and web-browsing. The life cycle of mobile phones as a broad product category is now at the mature stage, some would say saturated. But when individual product formats are examined, a pattern of continual development, launch, growth and eventual decline is evident. Mobile phone companies vision is to affect people, process and technology by enhancing workflow, improving access to knowledge, increasing the speed of business transactions and providing better modes of video watching feature. Some mobile phone companies are already using mobile applications to deliver video image to increased client matching feeling satisfaction. The mobile phone video watching speed convenient availability and price is factor to influence individual client to choose the mobile phone company's style video mobile or chooses another mobile phone to buy.

Some mobile companies have complex products that need to be maintained at the client's premises. Photocopies are a good example. The quality of field service and support is an obvious factor is establishing customer satisfaction as well as in building the kind of customer loyalty that leads to repeat business. The mobile companies have leveraged the potential of wireless support tools are gaining ground in the marketplace. I think mobile phone is not seen simply as a way to communication function. It ought to spend on carrying on researching and development on internet to deliver email message communication and it also needs to provide on line video watching entertainment service new features when every individual client is using every mobile phone company's different style of mobile phone if the mobile phone companies still wanted their mobile phones can sell to clients in this global mobile phone competitive market. Today, mobile phone is popular communication tool to every family. Due to beyond the rapid consumer adoption and usage of mobile phone is the opportunity mobile phone companies offer for brands to connect more meaningful and personally with consumers. Considering it every individual direct line and immediate connection with audience when who is leaving at home to communicate easily.

Most brands spend less than one percent of their marketing budget on mobile. The argument is that the one percent spend level is too low, given the fact that most consumers devote about 10% of their media attention to their mobile device.

During the 20 century, marketers employed mass-market media channels-Television , radio. The result was that brands created marketing massages that out of necessity had to appeal to a broad spectrum of consumers. It implied that watching video had been every person's habitual behavior everyday. If mobile phone can provide video watching feature to satisfy every client's seeing enjoyment. I think the individual client will choose to buy the mobile phone, which can provide video watching feature more than the mobile phone which can't provide video watching feature, even the individual client feels the owing video watching feature of mobile phone which price is higher than the lacking video watching feature of mobile phone. Because there are many people like to bring their mobile phones to watch video when who are leaving at home.

I shall suggest to do one marketing research of open to close survey method to new features, such as video on demand by whose mobile phone. The survey questions can be conducted , such as whether the client will determine to buy mobile phone with video feature more or who will determine to buy mobile phone without video feature more when the client need to buy one mobile phone to use; whether the client shall compare all different style of mobile phone with video feature which price, size, design and functions before the client determine to buy one mobile phone with video feature; whether what the factor is the most importance to influence the client choose to buy the mobile phone style with video feature, such as function, design, price, color, size, quality more durable use production of year; whether what factors influence the client to buy other companies' mobile phone with video feature, such as cheap price, unique indifferent design, attractive color, smaller size or larger size, production of year, whose friends or family introduction, advertisement promotion, convenient availability more durable use and quality; what kind of mobile phone with video feature, the client won't accept to use, such as screen picture is small size, image lacks clear color, too big size or too small size mobile phone feeling difficult to control . Hence, after any mobile phone had gathered their questionnaire researchers idea, then which can analyze whose data to carry on evaluating to estimate whether video features on mobiles demand on the difficult countries' consumer numbers. For example, every country sample of 100 people whose ages were between 10 ages to 20 ages segmentation group, a sample of 100 people whose ages were between 21 ages to 30 ages segmentation group, a sample of 100 people whose ages were between 31 ages to 40 ages segmentation group, a sample of 100 people whose ages were between 41 ages to 50 ages segmentation group, a sample of 100 people whose ages are between 51 ages to 60 ages segmentation group etc. If the 10 ages to 20 ages segmentation group had 50 people out of 100 people who prefer to buy video feature on mobile. It can estimate the country's this age group whose people numbers whether how many population shall prefer to buy video feature on mobile in the country. Hence, market survey research method can identify to measure every country's different age segmentation of client numbers who prefer to buy video feature on mobile clearly.

2. In terms of a new product development process, how could the development and launch of Tele point services have been improved in order to avoid the problems that were experienced ? What lessons can be learnt for the development of 3G (or 4G services)?

Adrian, P.(2012) showed that Hutchison is not new to taking big risks in the mobile phone market. It was behind the Rabbit network of semi-mobile Tele point phones launches in the UK in the 1980 years. These allowed callers to use a compact handset to make outgoing calls only, when they were within 150 meters of a base station, these being located in public places such as railway stations, shops, petrol stations, etc. As in the case of many new markets that suddenly emerge, operators saw advantages of having an early market share lead. Customers who perceived that one network was more readily available than any other would all other things being equal be more likely to subscribe to that network. Operators saw that a bandwagon effect could be set up to gain entry to the market at a later stage could become a much more expensive market challenger exercise. Such was the speed of development that the Tele point concept was not test marketed. To many, the development was too much product led, with insufficient understanding of buyer behavior and competitive pressures. Each of the four companies forced through their own technologies, with litter inclination or time available to discuss industry standard handsets which could eventually have caused the market to grow at a faster rate and allowed the operations to cut their costs. The Rabbit network came with the announcement by the UK government of its proposal to issue licenses for a new generation of personal communication networks, these would have the additional benefits of allowing both incoming and outgoing calls, and would not be tied to a limited base station range. By 2006 year, the next generation of mobile phone services were under development, with Japanese trials of 4G faster than 3G telecommunication service. 3G phones were also challenged by the development of alternative wireless access services, notably Wi Fi. Many companies, such as T-Mobile had began offering mobile Wi Fi services, which allow users to log on a local access points and gain access to their email and browse internet. Subscribers to VOIP telephone services could also effectively make the free phone calls from a Wi Fi access point. For many business travelers, using their laptop,

Wi Fi access seemed a more attractive and less expensive option than using a 3G phone connection to check for email. It was likely to become even more attractive, with development of longer range Wi Max services that extended beyond the very limited 50 meter or so range of Wi Fi. The pressure of 3G telecommunication services was intensified when the UK government announced in 2006 year that it would license the development of a national Wi Fi network.

It seems that 3G and 4G telecommunication service can be capable of speeds faster then Tele point Rabbit telecommunication in any places conveniently. It causes Tele point Rabbit telecommunication becomes obsolete to mobile to use. From 2003 year, mobile phones industry seemed that the new digital technology would be a third generation of mobile phones (3G). By 2008 year, work was well with the development of the next generation of fourth generation

mobile phone (4G) telecommunication service. In terms of a new product development process, the mobile companies need to consider the development and launch of Tele point services have been improved in order to avoid the problems that were experienced. The mobile product mix comprise range of mobiles that a company offers to the mobile market. Tele point service launching whether it is the individual mobile is with its core or secondary and augmented elements to influence consumers to buy mobiles essentially. I think the external factors, such as UK mobile phone companies whether which can sell the augmented mobiles or the secondary level mobiles or the core mobiles which can influence Tele point service demand, such as if the mobile company can only provide the core benefit, but it's style of mobiles which lacks the better characteristics in the secondary level to attract consumers, which shall reduce mobile sale numbers, features are such as mobile design, color, shape, reliability, texture, packaging , even if it lacks the augment level competitive effort, such as after sales service, brand name, credit facilities, speed of delivery and warranty. Thus, even Tele point service launching is useful to mobile buyers, if the consumers feel the mobile products prices are expensive and they are not valuable to attract them to buy mobiles. Tele point service is not the main factor to influence the buyers to choose to buy mobiles in UK mobile market when this mobile phones are launched to

sell in the beginning. The another factor is that Tele Point was new telecommunication service in 1980 in UK mobile telecommunication service market. There is likely to be a lot of promotional effort by Tele Point service to promote to mobile markets to secure sales. It is likely that the network of semi-mobile Tele point phones telecommunication service needs have high costs in the development of its service, costs that in the early stages may not be covered by revenue. Potential customers for a new network of semi mobile Tele point phones telecommunication service may be few and far between and therefore sales in early stages may be quite slow. This stage is known as the introduction stage. However ,Tele point phones telecommunication network service had this limitation. It only allowed callers to use a compact handset to make outgoing calls only, when they were within 150 meters of a base station, these being located in public places ,such as railway stations, shops, petrol stations, etc. If it's service proved popular, more people will show an interest and start purchasing it. However, due to many other mobile network telecommunication competitors who copied Tele point network telecommunication service technology to launch more fast speed and no location limitation and they can make incoming and outgoing calls both functions, even 3G or 4G telecommunication internet service is provided to mobiles. Hence, Tele point telecommunication network can not adopt to consumers demands.

Although, Tele point is the first network telecommunication service to adopt to handset in UK, but it handset network innovation can't identified as a source to mobile users' long term competitive advantages in this mobile phone network competitive market. Due to other telecommunication network companies can improve or revise to Tele point network service to launch more advance telecommunication service to provide mobile users to use more conveniently. Tele communication network fails due to mobile consumers useful demands are raising, its existing telecommunication service may no longer satisfy their needs, telecommunication technological change may make Tele point existing network service obsolete, telecommunication network service competitors can provide more convenient telecommunication nctwork to mobile phone users and the social and economic environment may have changed, creating new mobile users needs in the global mobile telecommunication network service market.

The development of information and communication technology (ICTS) with mobile can bring the benefits of within each of virtually all the world's people social communication, such as Japanese mobile phone focusing on 3G technology. Factors promoting it can be summarized as follows:

Deregulations by government/ mobile number portability and collocation; competition among carriers, such as introduction of new change plans; technological development, such as connection speed and contents and applications. Dynamic models are based out only on the assumption, such that carriers don't instantaneously adjust to satisfy their long term demand but also on network externalities. The Japanese mobile market has shown a remarkable growth with more than 106.2 million 3G subscribers and 4.4 million 2G as of Dec. 2009. The 3G diffusion rate accounts for 90% followed by that of Korea and this implies the market is almost saturated. Another remarkable transformation is found in its usage: Data communication exceeded voice services. Japanese 3G(4G) mobile phone originally had much variety of functionality other than voice service, being based on supply and demand side of the services: The founder is 3G technology which enabled new services, such as m-commerce and e-entertainment while the latter is due to existence of consumers who are willing to utilize various services. Although, the global mobile phone market has reached to the saturation stage and the growth rate of subscribers has been slowing down. Moreover, the recent development is found in the fact that data communications exceeds traditional voice communication and being the first phenomenon in the world. However, the effects of price elasticity and product differentiation of various carriers and network externalities increase the demand for mobile phone. Hence the technological innovation , such as electronic payment, high speed access and consumers' attitude toward entertainment and m-commerce are important factors for the success of 4G telecommunication service need is more than 3G telecommunication service need to every mobile phone users popularly. Moreover, new business models including a flat rate charging plan can play an increasing important role. Operators under these circumstances are confronted with competition due to the short product life cycle and the pressure to differentiate. Although, 2 G networks are adequate for voice, there was a growing interest in shifting from 2G to 3G even 4G based on a number of important drivers. First, the higher speed of 3G technologies translates into added convenience, capacity and functionality for the user. Second, there is much excitement over adding internet protocol (IP) capability and hence internet access to the mobile phone. In developing 3G standards, international telecommunication union worked with regional organizations and industry associates to reduce a large number of initial proposals to a smaller number of global standards.

In accordance with the development of mobile technology services already provided on 2G mobile phone , such as upgraded and consumers needed not feel difficult when using those services including email services (electronic mail, phone mail and video mail), web access and download music, movie and game. Moreover, carriers provide their customers more innovative functions, such as video mail, video-clips, video phone , broadcasting type video program, walk navigation, ringing tone songs, high speed internet connection, digital television broadcasting etc. via 3G mobile phone. In short, 3G services add multimedia facilities to 2 G phone by allowing video, audio and graphic application. Since 2G mobile had technological limitation of networks and handsets data transmitted via 2G was mainly text when due to development of networks and handsets, pictures and flash moving pictures are available and some handsets enables to view HPS for personal computer. Google and Yahoo started mobile search engines. Thus, 3G mobile becomes platform to use mobile contents, such as games and mapping services etc. Data communication , such as viewing web showed remarkable increase in 3G mobile phone, but monthly changes also increase and this became serious problem. In case of the internet in fixed communications, the flat rate changes are already introduced.

In addition, mobile carriers don't adjust to satisfy clients' long term demands and than dynamic model approaches are available . Especially, network externality or network effect has to be considered in telecommunication. Mobile telephone is the most widely used form by communication in the world today. Mobile communication boost the earnings of many users change the local economy and even significantly, raise the GDP of many countries. The mobile phone has a number of benefits but there is a huge gap in 3G mobile phone why there is the case only two countries . Japan and Korean have more 3G than 2G subscribers. Similarly, why do leading nations like the USA, UK and Germany have 3G pcnctration rates of less than 30%?

The conclusion, we obtained technological innovation were achieved first, than based on this various service innovation were followed. It should stress that the former includes innovations in handsets as well as those relates to networks and IP technologies. The diffusion on new services depends on how they meet clients preference and needs, but behind services innovations those always technological innovations. On the other hand, some other social backgrounds, such as consumer's attitudes, economies and businesses systems are required. For example, the Japanese and later other service providers solved the first start up problem for mobile internet (mobile internet uses 3G with entertainment content that was supported by a micro-payment system) . In conclusion, Tele Point telecommunication service failure was due to it felt it was the telecommunication service provider to Unite Kingdom people to use mobile, it believed UK people, even any countries‘ people ought only chose to use its telecommunication service monopoly. So, in this mobiles market, it did not continue to develop and launch its telecommunication technological service. However, due to its telecommunication service had geographic location distance limitation and out calling only limitation to every mobile UK and overseas users in different countries. Hence, many mobile users who would feel inconveniently. However, then other telecommunication service providers copies it's telecommunication technology to launch and research to develop 2G, even, 3G and 4G telecommunication technology, its competitors can provide no geographic location distance limitation and in calling and out calling both to every mobile user who can use conveniently. Finally, Tele Point telecommunication service was not accept to choose to use to its old mobile customers popularly, even the new mobile customers would choose to use any telecommunication service providers, due to which telecommunication service could give more advantages to compare it's telecommunication service.

If Tele Point telecommunication could spend time and technology to continue to launch to improve its telecommunication communication time speed, raised incoming call function and reduced no geographical location distance limitation difficulties (weaknesses). I believe that Tele Point telecommunication ought

attempt to continue to launch to improve its weaknesses of such as above weaknesses to adapt mobile consumers' demand easily, then it ought continue to keep its competitive position in this global telecommunication market till to nowadays.

3. Consider how the launch of 3G services in a less developed country with a less sophisticated telecommunications infrastructure may differ from a launch in a western developed county?

The growth has 3G telecommunication service in less developed country risk for the companies involved, especially where new technological displace the technology which went before them, calling for ever increasing capital investment, and no chance of a return from customers until long after the initial investment has been made in new capacity. Mobile phone companies need to predict the less developed countries, such as Africa country which has how many people who need mobile phone usage whether Africa has high businessmen who can support place, promotion, people and service to assist mobile phone companies to launch 3G or 4G telecommunication service. I think mobile phone companies need to let Africa country people to know mobile phone 3G telecommunication service technology is as the key to a whole new world of mobile telephone in which the mobile phone would be positioned not just as a device for voice communication, but a vital business, leisure, and information tool. So, mobile phones can assist Africa people to communicate in any places conveniently. A less developed country is a planned economy, the government makes all decision for society. Producers only make what they are instructed to make. The main benefits are that most workers are employed and most people enjoy a similar basic lifestyle. The problems cause to launch 3G mobile telecommunication service include that a planned economy gives little capacity for development, so growth and investment is limited, the infrastructure is usually under-developed as government spends on other areas, such as defense, wages are state controlled, so people have less motivation to perform at higher levels, mobile charges are fixed by government, consumers often can't afford luxury products, such as computers or mobile pones which are taken for granted in developed countries. Otherwise, a western developed country is in market economies (also known as free enterprise), the government's role is limited to providing legislation to protect businesses and consumers and making sure or organization restricts competition. It also provides essential services (like policy defense) and ensures the developed country's money supply is stable . Thus, businesses are motivated by profits to make products that clients will buy. Customers' demand for products and services affects the levels of supply and the pricing, if clients don't less be more efficient or produce on alternative product. For example, During 2003 year, the Hong Kong based Hutchison Whampoa became the first company to launch a 3G service in the UK, with its 3G telecommunication network. The launch was accompanied about the wireless internet and video capabilities. The world was going to be transformed by streaming of video and football matches live to customers' mobile phones and a whole new world of mobile advertising media would open up. However, launching 3G or 4G mobile telecommunication service to developed country , such as United Kingdom or less developed countries, such as Africa , I think the mobile phone companies need to consider what kinds of needs are the country people who prefer to get needs mostly. UK is a developed country, the people will need to get video entertainment, internet extra service from their mobile. Otherwise, Africa is a less developed country, the people live very far. It seems that location technology was value added data services. Even the emergency services stood to benefit from 3G's ability to precisely pinpoint a caller's location. By 2004 year, 60 per cent of calls to the UK emergency services were made mobile, but in instances callers did not know exactly where they were and ambulances and fire brigades only had very approximate locations. A less developed country is developing economy . It often face great difficulties in improving its economy. For example, in a planned economy, assets like land or property are owned by government. Individuals and businesses are not used to make decisions and operating to make a profit. Developing economy likes a less developed Africa country may also be market economy. But share features, such as the population lives on very low incomes, poor infrastructure , such as transport (roads or railways) or local government, poor communication systems, low levels of basic health and education and a low gross national product (GNP). Over 75% of the country's workforce is in agriculture which can be affected by the climate. Telephone landlines are scarce, expensive and difficult to install . It has less bank branches which are based in cities and tourist areas. Many Africa people are self employed business people, such as small farmers. The impact of mobile telecommunication technology on developing countries. The connectivity provided by mobile phone technology supports economic development. Its impact on a developing country likes Africa country has been extremely positive. Many families live in remote areas of the countryside . Installing landlines over those distances is expensive and difficult families are often separated as the main earners are forced to live in order to earn enough to keep their families. Many are self-employed small farmers or trades people such as plumbers and builders. For small business, better access to mobile technology means that who can advertise to a wider audience and don't have to rely for work on word of mouth. They can be sure that clients can contact them with ease. Due to far remote distance between houses and mobile phone companies, to launch in less developed county, any a mobile company must need a mobile network is quick and easy and secure to install and less expensive than landlines. For example, in a less developed country as Africa country, any mobile phone companies need to provide 3 G telecommunication service to any customers when who go to an accredited shop and in return for cash which has credit registered on their mobile to pay rather difficult than a pay as developed country mobile clients top up their mobile card. So developed countries mobile clients must pay their charge more convenient to compare to developing country mobile clients. Hence, mobile phone companies need to locate mobile card payment stores in developing country, such as Africa country's petrol stations, supermarkets and retail bases stores places. Hence, any mobile phone companies ought need to spend more capital expenditure to launch rapid commoditization of 3G or 4G telecommunication equipment and rising separation of network and service provisioning are pushing the operators to adopt multiple strategies with network infrastructure sharing in the core and radio access networks to improve network costs to a less developed country, such as Africa country more than a developed country, such as Hong Kong country. However, Africa is a potential mobile phone market. Due to limited land line availability, the cell phone is becoming Africa's computer of choice. Never before has a technological innovation been adopted as quickly as the introduction of cell phones in developing countries. Africa county mobile market will be larger to compare to fixed telephone lines, broadband, computer in home telecommunication markets. By international telecommunication union (2011) source indicated that global mobile usage, 2011 yr. of mobile subscriptions per 100 inhabitants statistic, Africa region had 53, Asia & pacific had 74, America had 103 and Europe had 120 inhabitant numbers. It implies Africa, less developed country had the least inhabitants to compare to any developed countries, so its mobile market will be large (Sullivan, 2007). In conclusion, extensive cell phone networks already are in place throughout the developing countries. These networks constitute and infrastructure providing clear solutions to many problems with building mobile transaction systems. These networks are not exist, but the majority of those in these nations, such as Africa country now uses cell phones for conventional voice communication and text messages to availability of inexpensive handsets and reasonable industry pricing structures. The features of mobile phones transaction systems in developing countries, include interface, network type, date, storage, power source for recharging cell phone, telecommunications provider, financial institution transactions of cash in/ out receipt service. So, due to its new technological development can raise its competitive effort, it will bring its advantage to raise its mobile sale price which won't reduce consumer number by behavioral economic method analysis.

CHAPTER THREE

Online market time consumer behaviors

Consumer behavioral factors influence theory
To research consumer behavior, it has different theory to explain why and how the consumer is influenced to make the choice by different factors. For example, utility theory,it explains that consumers make choices based on the expected outcomes of their decisions. They are viewed as rational decision makers and they only consider self interest.
Utility theory views consumer is as a " rational economic man". However, the factors influence consumer behaviors may include these activities, such as need recognition, information search, evaluation of alternatives, the building of purchase intention , the act of purchasing choice, consumption and finally disposal. Hence, it seems that all the consumer's activities in whose purchase processes. They will influence their choice. For example, when the property purchase consumer , he plans to research different kinds of properties information concern price, location, housing areas, room numbers, building facilities and environment facilities. He will find some sample target properties information to make comparison in order to decide to buy which of property is the most suitable to satisfy his living need.
However, it is not only one activity for the property purchasc buycr in his decision making process. It also include evaluation of alternatives activitiy when he ensures the accurate property information number in order to evaluate whether which one of all these property choices is the most suitable one. Hence, it explains that property information research and evaluation of alternatives both activities are needed to spend much time for this property buyer. If he does not plan to find one property to live in short time, it is possible that he can spedn one month, even more than one

month or more than three months time to do the only property information gathering activity.
Hence, it seems that time factor is not the main factor to influence the property buyer to do property purchase decision immediately. Otherwise, if the property buyer plans to find one new property to live within one month. Then, time factor is possible one important factor to influence this property purchase chocie decision. For example, if he felt that he needs more time to spend to gather information concerns the large house area size and the properties have more than three bathrooms and/or bedrooms properties information. Then, he will be possible not to find any this kinds of all property information. So, it means that all these properties won't be his choice. It is because long time property information gathering activity factor influnce.
I assume that the property buyer is a economic man and he does not spend much time to do the property information gathering activity. So, this kind of property needs him to spend long time to gather properties inforation in order to make this kind of properties comparison. Moreover, because he expects to live one new property within one month. So, he only chooses the properties, they have less than three bedrooms and/or bathrooms to gather sample properties information in order to make property purchase decision within one month. Hence, the time variable factor can only influence the property purchaser when he/she needs to make decision to buy one new property to live in the short time. If some kinds of properties choices number has a lot and the property buyer feels to let that he/she must need to spend long time to find the suitable properties number to make evaluation alternatives comparison behavior.
Then, the time variable limiting pressure factor will be possible the main factor to influence the property buyer's choice in order to make the most suitable kind of property purchase decision. Hence, it is one case example of how time limiting pressure factor can influence consumer purchase choice decision, such as property purchases market case. The reason explains why the property buyer needs to spend time to do property information gathering. I assume that general property buyer behave rationally in the economic sense. They won't only believe property agent individual property photos advertisement , it concerns where the property location is and facility etc. information on property photos in order to evaluate whether the property price is reasonable to pay. Generally, property buyers need to attempt to gather property information and visit the different actual

property locations to make choice. So, general property consumers would have to be aware of all the available different kinds of properties consumptin options from themselves properties information gathering and the properties agents' verbal properties introduction both be capable of correctly rating each property alternative and the available to select the optimum course of the final property purchase action.

Hence, in the property purchase and sold market, limiting time pressure factor will be important influential factor to decide whether the kinds of properties will be option to some property buyers when they feel need to find one suitable property to buy in short time. Otherwise, in some food consumption market , time limiting pressure factor will not be the main factor to influence consumer option. Such utility theory indicates consumers are as one rational economic man, whom do not expect to spend much time to do any options evaluation decision making.

However, in coffee market, buying a coffee comes almost automatically and does not need much information search. Hence, time limiting pressure factor won't one main factor to influence coff consumer to choose to buy the kind of coffee to drink. However, there are other factors to influence coffee consumers' kind of coffee drinking option from cultural, social, personal or psychological factors. So, coffee taste producer can follow these factors to estimate how coffee consumers might behave in the future when making any kinds of coffee making purchasing decisions.

Firstly, social factor can affect coff consumer behavior significantly. Every coffee consumer has someone around influencing his/her coffee buying decisions. The important social factors include reference groups, family, role and status , e.g. when the coffe buyer has high income job and his friends have good educational level and high income. Then, he will compare his reference group, such as his friends' coffee buying behavior choosing which kinds of coffee taste to drink in habits or lifestyles. If he chooses the kind of coffee taste to drink, its price is cheaper to compare his friends' drinking coffee tastes. Then, he may be influenced to follow his friends to drink the same kinds of coffee taste in order to keep their same social status and role between him and his friends.

Secondly, the coffee consumers will be influenced how to choose which kinds tastes of coffee to drink by personal factors, such as his age, life cycle state, occupation, economic situation , lifestyle and personality and self-concept. Age related factors are such as taste in food, e.g. the kinds of coffee taste. Although, coffee price is cheap, but if the coffee consumer's income is more and he/she can often spend to buy different kinds of taste coffees to drink. Then, his/her income level will have much purchasing power to influence his/her purchasing behavior. Hence the coffee consumer's frequency of consumption of different kinds of coffee taste drinking choice behavior will represent whether his/her income level is high or low in possible. For example, the consumer needs to go to automatic coffee shop to buy at least three cups or more different kinds of high class good taste coffee brands to drink per week. Although, these high class coffee brands' prices are higher than the low class of coffee brands. But the coffee consumer still only buys any one of these kinds of high class brands' coffee taste to drink. Hence, it seems that this coffee consumers ought have high income to let hims to buy at least three cups of high class brand of coffee taste to drink from automativ coffee ship per week.

So, income factor can influence the coffee consumer to choose either coffer purchase from supermarket or coffee drinking at automatic coffee shop. If the coffee consumer only chooses to buy coffee from supermarket, due to the bottles of different kinds of brand coffee can provide more different tastes of coffees choices from shelves to let him to buy to drink at home. So, it seems that the coffee consumer's income level is low in general. Otherwise, if the coffee consumer only chooses to go to automtic coffee shop to buy the high class brands of coffee tastes to drink at least thre times or more per week. It may mean that the coffee consumer has high income level to support him/her to often go to automatic coffee shop to buy different kinds of high class coffee tastes to drink frequently every week. Som high or low income level factor can influence every coffee consumer individual drinking coffee behavioral options.

Moreover, when the coffee consumer is younger coffee consumer will be possible to buy much coffee to drink. Because younger age people can accept to drink coffee habitually more than older age people. Also, it is possible that younger peopler feel often drinking coffee behavior will help them to bring more health feeling and /or raising nervous to learn , due to they need often to go to schools to study. Otherwise, older age people feel often drinking coffee behaviors won't help them to bring more health and they do not need to raise nervous to learn.

Finally, even, cultural difference factor will influence coffee consumers number fo any countries. For example, western countries'people like to drink any kinds of coffee tastes traditionally. Asia countries' people like to drink any different kinds of teas tastes traditionally. So, different kinds of teas tastes will be asia people's traditional drinking substitute to replace different kinds of coffee tastes more easily. Hence, culture difference will be one factor to influence asia coffee buyers number. So, it seems that time limiting pressure factor won't influence coffee consumers' coffee taste choices to different kinds of high class or low class brands, visiting coff shops or visiting supermarkets choices, frequent or not frequent coffee drinking behaviors.

How and why time limiting pressure influences consumer choice

Can consumer buying decisions be influenced by time limiting pressure. For these three situations, they will influence consumer hoe makes different buying decision, e.g. in the little time available, but the consumer needs to do more effort needed to choose to buy which kind of product among variety kinds of product choice or in a moderate amount of time available, or a considerable amount of time available. In this first situation, the consumer can not real attempt to find any weaknesses or unique characteristics of the products, because it has no enough time to allow whom to choose. So, his/her product evaluation won't be th most accurate to satisfy his/her needs because little time can only allow him/her to find some weaknesses of the products. Otherwise, in the final situation, because the consumer has a considerable amout of time to allow him/her to attempt to find the weaknesses and/or strengths characteristics of the products choice. So, he/she ought do the more reasonable or accurate evaluation of these products to choose the most effective economic beneficial product to buy. Thus, it seems that time limiting pressure factor can influence the consumer to make more rational or more reasonable economic beneficial consumption decision making to buy the product or consume the service.

Thus, a consumer buying decision will require these situations to do buying decisions, they may include either little time and conscious effort or a moderate amount of time and effort or a considerable amount time and effort. The products may include cheap products/services , e.g. fruit, DVD, university courses, computers, facial services, surgeries, sport shoes, reference books, soft drinks, magazines as well as expensive products/ services, e.g. cars, houses, luxury goods, e.g. jewellery, female hand bags, holiday travelling entertainment. So, any expensive or cheap products or services, the consumer will need to spend either little or moderate or considerable amount time to do gathering information about the different kinds of products or services in order to find which brand of product or service can bring more economic benefit when he/she chooses to use the product or consume the service. He/she will compare his/her preference sample brands limiting number of products or services choices to decide to buy the brand of product or consume the brand service easily. However in the consumer's consuming decision making process, he/she will need to spend either little or moderate or a considerable amount of time to do the evaluation and choice consumption behavior. It means that time limiting pressure factor will influence the consumer how to make consumption choice consequently.

What are the impacts of reduced branding on consumer choice and time limiting pressure to influence consumer behavior? When one consumer needs to choose products to buy one in a time limiting pressure consumption environment, when branding on packaging is reduced, e.g. the brand of product has 10 different style of packages to let consumer choice, but it reduces to only 5 different style of packages to let consumer choice. How does it influence the consumer decision making when the consumer has little time to allow to choose these 5 different style of packages ? For example, when the consumer expects to spend only 10 minutes to choose any one style of package to buy drom this brand product. Currently, this brand of produxt has reduced different style of packages number from 10 to 5. Do you feel that the consumer will feel easy to do decision making to choose to buy the most attractive style of package product from this brand's 5 different style of packages choices? Is 10 minutes consumption choice time enough to let the consumer to make final purchase decision from these brand's 5 different style of packages choice? Will the time limiting pressure be reduced , due to this brand's 10 style packages are reduced to 5 style packages to let the consumer to choose within the 10 minutes expected limiting consumption choice time.

It is one interesting psychological consumption behavior to research whether the brand's reducing different style of packages number factor will influence the consumer to do the decision making in the short time in the time limiting pressure environment. For toothpaste, shapmo products example, if the brand of these products' style packages choice is reduced to 5 style packages from 10 style packages choice. When one consumer finds the brand of toothpaste or shampo has only 5 style packages on the shelves in supermarket. If the consumer has moderate or considerate amount time to let him/her to choose these both kinds product any one style of packages to buy. The 5 style packages to these both inds of products will be impossible to satisfy the consumer's choice need because he/she haas much time to stay in supermarket to choose. Otherwise, if the consumer has little time to allow to stay in the supermarket , e.g. ony 10 minutes. Then, he/she expects to spend only 10 minutes consumption choice time to do buying decision making within 10 minutes. These both kinds of the brand's products, its styl of packages choice number is reduced to 5, it is possible to satisfy the consumer's choice need to buy this brand of product either toothpaste or shampoo and both of thee brand of products to be chose to buy in the supermarket. So , the reducing style of package number to let consumer choice will be seem to let the conumer to do buying decision making in the limiting time pressure consumption environment.

In fact , package is such a visual to influence consumer decision making in the short time or personal limiting time choice process. If the product has more attractive package design, the it can bring more attention effort to influence the consumer to choose to buy the product in the short time information transfers to influence the consumer decision making to choose to buy more easily , when he/she is active in communication process. So, package, communicating with consumer in the selling place , has become an essential factor to influence the choice of consumer.

Scientific researches have proved that package decisions can attract consumer attention, transfer the desirable information abou tthe product, position , the product in consumer conscious, differentiate and identify of among similar kinds of products. In that way elements of package influence consumer decision making process and can determine the choice of consumer and the package itself can become more competitive advantage.

However it is not absolute that the brand of product has more package choices, it must have more customers to choose to buy its product. For example, there are two brands of shampoo in the supermarket shelf. One brand shampoo has 5 different style of packages and 5 different fruit productive elements to cause similar fresh fruit smells to attract consumers to buy. Another brand shampoo has 3 different style of packages and 3 different fresh fruit smells to attract consumers to buy in the same shelf location also. When one supermarket customer has little time to expect to stay in the supermarket, e.g. he expects only to stay the supermarket maximum to 15 minutes. he expects to buy one bottle shampoo and meats and fruits and vegatables within 15 minutes. Hence, he expects only to spend about 5 minutes to choose one brand of shampoo product as well as he demands to spend maximum 10 minutes to buy other foods within 15 minutes. When he stays in the shampr shelf location, he finds only two brands of shampoo products are displayed on the same shelf location. One brand of shampo has 5 different style packages to let him to choose, but he feels that these 5 diffeent style packages are not very attractive. Otherwise, the another brand of shampo has only 3 different style packages to let him to choose, but he feels that the 3 different style packages are very attractive. Due to he feels time causes pressure to choose these two brands of shampoo immediately. So, he does not want to spend more time more than 5 minutes to choose on brand of shampoo to buy. He will be influenced by the brand of different styles of packages more attraction to influence his buying decision making obviously. So, whether the shampoo brand's package is attractive or not, it will influence the consumer's buying decision making to choose either to buy the brand's shampo product in preference.

So, the more packages choice to the brand's product which may not mean that it has high opportunity to influence consumers' attention. Otherwise, the attractive package element if more important to compare right number of packages choices. Consumer package can influence these elements, e.g. colour, size, imageries, graphics, materials, smell, brand name, producer/ country, information, special offers. Of the brand of products can have much attractive elements. Then, it can attract consumers to choose to buy the brand's attractive package products in short time decision making process, such as perception of needs, search for information , evaluation of alternatives, decision making, behavior after purchase. Such as supermarket case, I assume that any supermarket consumers do not expect to spend much time to choose which brand of product is the most suitable or earning more economic benefit to buy when they need to stay the shelf to need spend much time to select which brand of product to buy in the supermarket. Because in general, supermarket consumers ought plan to buy more than one kind of product or food, even more usually. So, limiting time pressure factor will influence their decision making. Similarly, as my explanation indicates why although, the product had attractive package elements and its has many packages number choices, but it does not mean that it can win the similar product which has not more attractive packages, even it has more packages choices number to let supermarket consumers to choose. So, an attractive package element factor will have more influential and potential to cause supermarket consumers to choose to buy it in the supermarket limiting time pressure consumption environment.

How the time consumption pressure factor influences irrational consumption decision making

When one consumer has a large number of options, he/she will feel time pressure to cause whose accurate and reasonable evaluation. Then, the personal time limiting pressure factor will bring these questions: How does the time limiting pressure influence the consumer evaluation? Will the consumer personal limiting time pressure bring advantages and / or disadvantages in whom consumption decision making? How to help the consumer to solve short time decision problem when he/she encounters extreme time pressure an dchoice overload?

I shall assume every consumer is general one economic man. He/she feels time is important, he /she does not want to spend much time to choose one brand of product to buy among a number of brands of products choices. I also assume that any consumers decision making satisfaction, which is based on search until they found a sufficiently good item, or run not of time. So, it seems that which the consumer needs to buy one kind of product, but the product has a lot number of different brands to let the consumer to choose. The consumer ought need to spend much time to make choice decision making. However, consumer is one economic man, he/she ought not to search all different brands to decide whether which brand of product can bring the much economic value or utility value to choose to buy. So, in general, consumers will only choose sample brands of products to decide to buy the satisfied brand of product. For example, when the consumer needs to buy one television. The television has 20 brands of similar televisions to let he to choose. He will not spend much time to search these similar 20 televisions information. He will only gather sample 10 to 15 or less different brands of televisions to compare what their strengths and weaknesses, unique characteristics. Then, he will make decision to choose to buy the best television from these sample televisions. Hence, in general, consumers will feel time pressure when they feel need to spend much time to choose a lot different brands of similar products. Because they feel time is not enough to let they can do other important matters when they need to spend much time to do search information behavior when they need to buy any products ususally. Hence, it is general consumers psychology that they will feel real choice under time pressure and choice overload, when they have too much a lot of similar brands of products to let them have opportunity to

choose to make decision making to buy only one brand of product.
However, when a brand of product is familiar and given its simplicity and familiarity to general consumers' acknowledgement. It will have perference advantage to attract or influence consumers' attention or consideration. So, when the market has similar different brands of products are available to let consumers to choose. The largest choice set is not large enough to create overload to influence the brand's sale when consumers need to spend much time to choose these different brands similar products to buy. Because when the brand's any products are familiar and given its simplicity and familiarity to general consumers' knowledgement. Then, it can build utility confidence to influence general consumers , it will be preference sample brand of product to do buying making option. Hence, the brand's familiarity factor will influence general consumers' preference buying decision making option. So, any product manufacturers need to concern how to build its brand familiarity to let many consumers to acknowledge in order to raise its competitive effort. Raising brand's familiarity may be a good method to solve consumer individual choice under time pressure overload , because when the brand of product is preference sample brand to any consumers. It's sale opportunity will also be raised. So, it brings the question: How can the brand of products can cause general consumers' preference choice. For food example, food brands were more likely to choose the implicitly preferred brand over the explicitly preferred one when choices were made under time pressure.
Imagining one customer enters a supermarket 10 minutes before closing time. He failed to write up a shopping list. So, when the staff is preparing to close store at the night, the consumer hurry trys not to for set too many of the ingredients for dinner . What brands of products , he opts for, as he can choose from a variety of similar foods, but time is short and the staff is looking at the consumer impatienty? It is possible that the consumer will probably quickly decide in favor of the foods he likes best, pay, and leave the evening.
Hence, supermarket consumer's first time feeling to the brand of food will influence whom choice. One target category and one attribute category share same response key: Pleasant vs unpleasant feeing, if the supermarket consumer has pleasant feeling when he sees the food photos and touchs the package of the brand of food to feel pleasant in the short supermarket closing time. Then, his pleasant feeling will be chooses to buy the brand of food to eat. Thus, the consumer individual pleasant or unpleasant feeling

factor will influence whom consumption choice, such as this supermarket closing time pressure consumption.

In fact, many factors may influence whether consumer behavior is under more or less control. Hunger may influence control in the domain of eating behavior . So, such as the supermarket will close soon,it has store closing time pressure to influence the consumer needs hurry to make choice decision to buy food. If the consumer feels more hungry, he will not spend much time to find the right food to buy. He will be influenced by the different brand's food packages whether which brand of food package can bring a more pleasant to let him to feel, when he touchs and sees the brand of food package. He won't spend time to search whether the different kinds of brands of foods have how much different health elements because the supermarket will close store soon. So, he only depends his individual pleasant feeling to make final food purchase decision. If he feels all of the kinds of brands foods are unpleasant food packages when he sees and touchs them first time as well as he does not feel much hungry. Then, it is possible that he won't choose to any one food to eat. He will choose to go to restaurant to get dinner to replace buying food to cook to eat dinner at home at the night.

The another case is that time pressure concerns how on choice of information source impacts purchase decisions. When the consumer who buys one product , he needs to use the same number of information sources to search the product's information regardless of time pressure. Because he has more available time, he devotes more time , but only to selected the right sources to search information about the product. He will mostly use marketing dominant sources, e.g. magazine. he feels magazine can give more accurate information concerns to the product's good or bad quality real more reasonable and fair evaluation to let the consumer to acknowledge. so, when the consumer has much time to choose to buy which brand of product is the most best choice. He will buy magazine to find information. He believes magazine has more fair evaluation to different brands of product. It won't mislead consumers to make wrong decision making. Hence, in general, when consumers have much time to find information source to search which brand of product is more value to buy. They will attempt to buy consumer magazine to acknowledge whether the different brands of product , which have unique characteristics, strengths or weaknesses in order to compare them to make more accurate evaluation to choose to buy which brand of the kind product. When they have no time pressure to influence their choice process time to be shortened or reduced. Otherwise, these consumers will depend on newspapers, television, radio advertisments information sources when they feel time pressure controls their consumption choice decision making process time to be shortened or reduced. Hence, time pressure will be possible to influence consumer individual information source channel choice.

Time pressure consumption decision
making process characteristics

How we can predict or know the consumer time pressure in whom decision making process? Will it bring advantages or disadvantages to influence the businessmens' benefits? I shall indicate some different consumption situations or environments to explain what will be impacted to sale number is increased or decreased to businesses when the consumer feel time pressure to avoid whom behavioral consumption to the product or the service.

Firstly, I shall explain that what effects of product popularity and time pressure on online shopping behaviors are . Electronic ecommerce is popular to any countries, in special, US, UK, China large areas countries, because when one customer feels need to spend one hour even more time to catch any transportation tool to arrive the shop to buy the kind of product. Then, due to far distance reason, he/she will choose to apply internet to buy the kind of product . If the seller has website to let the consumers to choose online shopping. However, it seems that online shopping behavior can reduce the consumer individual time pressure, when he/she feels need to catch any kinds of transportation tool to arrive the shop to buy the product. Moreover, when the consumer can turn on home computer to enter its website to choose the styles of the kind of products, which one is the most situable to choose. He/she can spend time to search the different styles kinds of product information to compare and evaluate which brand of product will b whose purchase choice easily at home.

Hence, in psychological view, he/she can feel that spending time to search information from internet behavior which is more valuable and it can bring more economic benefit to make final purchase decision more than the behavior of spending long time to catch any transportation tools to visit the shop. Moreover, it is possible to bring failure risk that he/she wastes time to catch any transportation tools to visit the shop if he/she can not find any one of suitable product(s) to choose to buy. Hence, it seems the online shopping can influence the consumer reduced time pressure and wastes time to do any shopping decision.

This is online shopping's attractive strengths to the consumers when they need to spend long time to catch any kinds of transportation tools to visit the shop or when the consumer feels hurry to do other important matters, he/she can not allow himself/herself to spend long time to do his/her visiting the shop behavior. Moreover, another online shopping's advantage is that product popularity can be perceived by examining the information presended on websites. For example, research on onlin reviews confirms the review quantity presented with products become positively influences to consumers' purchase intention and it can persuade the online visitor can make decision to buy the product when he/she has enter the seller's online website to find the most suitable product to choose to buy more easily. Hence, it seems that it is more easy to persuade the online visitor to make final purchase decision more than visiting the shop , when the online visitor can attempt to do the click mouse behavior to enter the seller's online shop, such as website. Then, he/she will be influenced to view the seller's different kinds of colourful and attractive product pictures from the seller's wesite.

Consequently, it has much opportunity to persuade the consumer to do the final purchase decision. if the seller's website is attractive to persuade him/her to visit its website to find any new products more than five times, even tem times or every weak several times , even day one time frequently visiting behavior from internet channel. Hence, due to internet is convenient tool to let consumers to find any product informatons from the seller's website at home or public library , computer, or mobile phone. Consumers must find any product informations any time in any places easily. So, online shopping can reduce any consumers' time pressure to visit any shops to expect to achieve final consumption decision aim in possible.

Thus, it seems that online shopping method can influence consumers to feel time saving and time presure reducing consumption both advantages more than visiting shops' shopping method when the consumer is living far away from the shop. When the consumer feels that he/she is experiencing situational time pressure, then, he/she will respond well to seek another time saving situational consumption environment. So , it explains when one consumer feels he/she has no much time to catch long time transportation tool to visit the shop on the day. When he/she has computer at home, he/ she will attempt to type the shop name to research whether it has online shopping platform service from internet. Because he/she does not want to spend one hour, even more time to catch transportation tool to arrive the shop, when he/she can't walk to the shop in short time. Even, he/she may feel online shopping behavior won't influence his/her eating , sleeping, or recreational time to be reduced at home or any places , when he/she can behave the online shopping behavior at home or any where conveniently.

Consequently, promoting online shopping is as a time-saver is likely to be effective for these experiencing situational time pressure. Those with situational pressure would almost certainly welcome anything that would reduce their activity level and the demands on their time. In fact, there is really no adult learning method for store shopping because it is something everyone learns to do from early childhood. But for many adult consumers, they feel have interest to learn how to use internet and web to shopping. Some adult will feel interest and it is value to learn how to use internet channel to anticipate the complexity of shopping online. For example, Super Walmart cheap frocery store that carries many thousands of products and brands to let online shoppers won't feel confused when viewing its online merchant's home page with only a few menu items and links from its website. So, Super Walmart website can let online shoppers to feel difficult that they can save much time to enter any merchants' home page . They only need to view the Super Walmart's website ,then they can find any preference cheap grocercies to compare and evaluate which one(s) is (are) value to buy. So, Super Walmart's website can let global cheap grocery online shoppers feel it can help them to save time to find any merchant's products from internet conveniently. Consequently, online shopping will be one popular time saving consumption channel to reduce time pressure to some consumers nowadays.

Secondly, I shall explain that what determines purchase decisions for airline tickets when the traveller fees time stress. When a travelling planner has no enough time to prepare whose travelling journey, whether the time stress will influence he/she feels decision difficulties and frustration, when it will cause he/she needs to gather significant amounts of information to lead to make to choose which airline ticket is the most right choice? How and number of airline options and time pressure influence the airline ticket buyer's purchase decision?

However, there are both kinds of time pressures to influence the airline ticket buyer's airline choice decision, they focus on either real decision deadlines (physical time), such as the journey beginning day is any day of this week or tomorrow or subjective feeling of pressure with time (sense of urgency or psychological time), such as the traveller expects that he/she fears all airlines' all seats are full booked in this month. Moreover, he/she can plan to catch air plane to travel next month. So, he/she will attempt to gather any airlines' tickets prices, flight day and time and destination arrival and weather information in this month to avoid that it is too late to delay his/her next month travelling plan.

Hence, it seems that the effect of number of airlines choices and air tickets purchase deadlines (physical time limit) will influence how the traveller or air ticket buyer's purchase decision using secondary data to search of airline ticket. for example, if the traveller felt time is no enough to let him/her to go to travel agent to enquire any airlines' air tickets prices and seats and date and time air plan departure available time to concern the traveller's destination choice. Then, he/she will be probable to choose to buy electronic-ticket (e-ticket) from internet. If he/she has computer to link internet to gather any airlines' flying date and time and seat available information at home easily. Hence, it seems that one time pressure traveller will be probable to choose e-ticket purchase at home in preference. If the airline can provide online e-ticket purchase option to the time pressure traveller. Due to the pressure time traveller feels closer to departure, the negative impact of number of airline options is not as strong when he/she can view the airline's website to find the flight date, time and seat available information to purchase e-ticket to prebook the date and time to departure the traveller's country and to arrive his/her travelling destination information from the airline's website channel at home or anywhere any time conveniently. Hence, travel agency can bring a positive relationship between airline number of options and pre-booking airline that immediate possibility. When the time pressure traveller hopes the airline can build the good interactive relationship between number of options and decision time limit (number of days till planned travel effort on e-ticket purchase probabilities. So, if the airline website can let the traveller to predict when date and time is accurate available to arrive whom frequently destination choice country as well as the e-ticket's real price , it is not e-ticket preductive price and the real seats number available, it is not the estimated seats number available on the departure time and date to the travelling or arrival country destination. Then, all of these online information to the airline, which will raise the e-ticket pre-booking purchase chance to let the e-ticket buyer to make whose final e-ticket purchase choice decisin to win

its e-ticket competitors easily.
Consequently, a real time e-ticket information can attract any time pressure e-ticket buyers to choose to buy its e-ticket (electronic airline ticket) more than visiting travel agent's paper airline ticket option when the travel feels hurry to buy airline ticket to travel in short time.

Reducing time pressure consumption
methods

How can sellers persuade consumers to choose to buy their products or consume their services in time pressure environment easily? It is a valuble research topic to concern how to know how consumer individual decision making to spend his/her available resources (time, money and efforts, or consumption relatd aspects) as well as how any why he/she chooses the preference brand to buy its any kind of products or consume its services, when he/she chooses to buy the brand of products or consume its services? Hence, marketers need to obtain an indepth knowledge of consumer buying behavior.
In any buying process, time factor will have about 10 % to 40 % to influence consumer decision. When the consumer feels hurry to consume, e.g. planning to go to travel, when he/she needs to choose to buy which airline's air ticket and what day and time is the right air ticket prebooking purchase decision right time choice; or enrolling which school to be choosed course to study decison, e.g. how long time is needed to be choose which school is the most suitable to provide the most suitable courses studying choce change; purchase warm clothes to wear in winter, when is the suitable time to choose to buy the cheaper warm clothers to prepare to wear in winter, e.g. Jan to Mar., April to June, July to Aug. month; when is the most suitable time to buy another new house to live, when the property consumer(buyer) has lived present house for long time, e.g. three years or more. All of these issues will include time factor to influence the consumer feels when he/she ought choose to buy the kind of product or consume the kind of service. However, the other factors will also include to influence his/her decision, e.g. family, friend relationship factor, advertising factor, social status factor, cultural difference factor, personal psychological need level or satisfactory level factor, young or old age factor, income level factor, economic environment factor, material enjoyable need factor etc. factors.
However, time pressure factor will be the consumer individual intrinsic (internal) psychological feeling factor, and it is the consumer individual

intrinsic feeling to judge whether when he/she ought spend some money to buy the kind ofcnew product or the kind of consume service (what time is the most reasonable or the most suitable time) to make purchase choice decision. However, when the consumer feels hurry to make purchase decision. So, he/she will not hope to spend more time to gather more information to compare and evaluate which one is the right brand of product tochoose to buy or the right service to consume among different brands of products or services. Otherwise, if the consumer has more time or he/she can make the decision to buy any brand of product. Then, he/she ought spend more time to gather more information to compare and evaluate which one is the most suitable product choice to buy or which one is the right service choice to consume. So, time pressure factor will have some influence to any consumers to make decision about what time is the suitable time to buy the kind of product or consume the service. For example, heater product is usually when winter weather time, the heater products need number ought increase in winter weather time or season. But, it is possible that the heater products need number won't increase in winter season / weather possible, when one country , there are many householders or families , they have one heater number at least at home. Then, it is possible that these householders or families won't have consumption desires to buy one more heater product to use in winter at home, because they have had one heater to use at home in winter. So , when the country has have many customers number, they are using the kind of heater products at homes. Most people own at least one heater number factor will have possible to influence enough time available to cause they do not feel hurry to buy any heaters to use at homes, so, their do not feel time pressure to buy any heaters in short time. Because they do not plan to buy the kind of product to use at home in short time when they have one heater product at least to use at homes in present.

Hence, it brings this question: How to attract or persuade the customers, they are using the kind of product to let they feel time pressure to make decision to buy another new or same brand of product to replace to use? The product's better quality , long durable time useful, brand loyalty and past good purchase experience factors will influence him/her to feel time pressure to need to buy another new product in short time. So,when the consumer feel time pressure to make decision to purchase, he/she will choose when is the most right time to gather information, search, select, use and dispose of another new product to replace the old product in the short

time.
Hence, the brand of product needs have good product motives, may be raised to the consumer's impluse, desires, considerations which make the buyer purchase the brand's new product to replace the present using product in order to achieve whose satisfactory needs to emotional product motives and rational product motives both. Moreover, persuading or encouraging the consumer feels he/she has real need to buy the kind of new product or replace the present old product (s), the brand of product marketer needs let the consumer feels these any one of nature of motive to raise his/her purchase decision desire in time pressure environment. The natures of motive may include: When the consumer feels desire for saving money, he/she will choose to buy it when the brand of product falls down, when he/she feels fear to be sickness, retirement, he/she will choose to buy insurance policy, when he/she feels pride, or high social status knowledgement, he/she will buy premium product , e.g. gold, expensive watch, car , when he/she feels fashion need, he/she will move house to live from rural to urban, or rural people imitate urban to learn to do their fashion living behavior, when he/she feels possession need, he/she will feel need to buy antiques for its future unique worth satisfactory feeling in possible, when he/she feels health need, he/she will choose to buy health foods, join memebership in health clubs, when he/she needs to enjoy comfortable feeling, he/she will feel need to buy micro-oven, washing machine to use at home, when he/she feels love and affection need, he/she will buy gift items to give to whose friends or families for presents in their birthday or lover day etc. special days to let they to feel happy. So, when the marketer can touch the consumer individual different nature of motives to satisfy his/her personal purchase feeling need and it can know how to influence them to feel that they have these any one of purchase motive needs in short time. Then, they will be persuaded to raise time pressure to make purchase decison to buy any kind of products in short time.
However, instead of attractive good product quality method can attempt consumers to make time pressure consumption behavior. The another method is brand loyalty building method, which can be attempted to encourage or persuade consumers to feel consumption desire need to make decision to buy the brand of any products in time pressure consumption environment. For example, when the consumers feel the brand is loyalty and it can build good image to his/her feeling , and this time pressure factor can inlfuence this brand of any products which has high discount

price to attract the consumer individual attention , e.g. familiar brand high class cars, the good confident house agent's high class houses, and the expensive and infrequently buying items, come under this category. When their prices are fallen down to sell cheaper , e.g. twenty per cent discount or more than twenty percent discount sale price than the other similar competitive brands' any products' normal prices. Then, it is possible to let these expensive items' consumers have high involvement and high feeling need in time pressure consumption environment. Because they assume that this discount sale price will be short time sale price, e.g. after three months or next month etc. short time discount sale price in short time period. Then, these expensive items' prices will be raised to the normal sale price, even higher price. so, they have time pressure feeling to feel that it is right time to make consumption decision in order to avoid to lose these low price purchase benefit in this unpredictive cheap discount price purchase items. so, if the expensive item marketer can build long time good brand loyalty relationship to consumers. Then, it will have much influential effort to persuade consumers feel consumption desires need by its any extensive items in the unpredictive short term discount period, due to they do not want to loss this large discount purchase price chance. So, short time discounted sale price, it is another method to persuade consumers to choose to buy the brand's any products in short time pressure consumption environment.

The another persuading time pressure consumption method is that it can let consumers to think more habitual buying the kind of products. products like stationery, groceries, food etc. fall under this category. For example, when the consumer fees the brand of any products ,he/she has habitual purchase experience, of he/she feels that the brand's any products won't sell in market temporary, even he/she can not buy it to use again. Then, it is possible to infuence him/her to feel immediate purchase need to buy a lot of product or food number to keep to use or eat later in the time pressure environment, e.g. the food consumer buys the brand of any breads to eat in supermarkets habitually, but in this moth, he/she watchs TV advertisement to be acknowledge this brand of any breads won't be bought from any supermarkets as soon as possible. Hence, it is possible to influence him/her to plan to make choice to buy a lot of number of this brand of any breads in order to keep the enough of this brand of breads number to eat later. So, this brand of any breads sale loss in supermarkets that will cause the habitual food consumers of this brand of breads, whom make consumption choice to buy a lot number of this brands any breads in short time suddenly. Because they are eating this brand of any kinds of breads habitually. They feel much eating need to lot number of this brand of any breads in short period, because it can satisfy their habitual taste needs of this brand's any kinds of breads. So, brand loyalty and habitual consumption to the kind of product or food , ehich will result simply from the habit and it can influence the consumers feel consumption need to buy the brand's any kinds of products or foods when they feel that they may not buy it again or they can not earn discount advantage after the short time. So, any one of these sale strategies will have possible to raise the consumer individual consumption desire to the brand of products in the short time pressure consumption environment. Also it needs to spend much time to gather information in order to make purchase decision, because the brand had built confidence to consumers when they feel this brand's any products or foods are better to compare the similar brands' any products or foods habitually. So, time pressure consumption environment will persuade them to feel consumption desire to buy this brand's any products or foods in short time. When, they fer that they can not buy any more for this brand's any kinds of products or foods or discounting price in this final short purchase time.

In conclusion, these factors can influence consumer behaviors to be changed to feel time pressure need to do purchase decision making behavior from encough time gathering information available feeling behavior. They have these same views, e.g. habits and routines are very influential, particularly for behaviors repeated daily in a semi-automatic fashion. The consumer's past purchas experience to the brand's products, positive or negative emotion to the brand's products, and the brand's familization, recognition are strong influence , the information available , it is the consumer's mind and the relative important information given to let the consumer knows form different advertisement medias matters for decision making, greating between pieces of information and can be influenced by personal psychological timing limited pressure, the consumer's comparison to differences in price or other characteristics, many pursue value (or in bargain), and compare to alternatives or past knowledge, consumer personal greater value on the immediate future and heavily disocunt future costs or savings to the brand of product, feeling simple and easy decision making process to the product , it can lead the consumer to avoid to spend long time to make purchasing decision and the consumer will easy to choose to buy the product when he/she feels have a loss value if he/she does not decide to buy the product in the short time. SO, it seems that when the marketer can motivate the consumer's consumption desire to feel saving money, promote health, avoid waste time and less nervous workload to gather information for comparison and evaluation alternatives aim. It is seen favorably by the consumer personal time pressure purchase decision making and sense of justice influence factors.

However, sociologists have categorised the motives for consumption behaviors in the short time by the fundamental consumption decision making needs or wants which they satisfy, e.g. having a clear understanding what benefits, characteristics, economic value to the brand's any products , feeling consumption decision making process is a leisure activity. These drivers for consumption behaviorw will either bring positive or negative to influence the consumer personal emotion, either owning enough time available or time pressure environmental impacts can be seen to influence whether the consumer feels he/she needs how long time to be spent to make comparison and evaluate alternatives in order to make final purchase choice in whom decision making process. Hence, the consumer himself/ herself time pressure consumption decision making feeling, it can bring positive purchase choice influence,when the marketer can build brand loyalty to let many consumers to feel in the market. Otherwise, if the marketer can not build brand loyalty to let many consumers to feel, but consumers feel time pressure to compare and evaluate its any products to other similar brands of products in the competitive market. Then, its products may be not the preference choices the many customers among the different brands of products choices. So, building long time brand loyalty relationship to satisfy consumers' needs, it will bring positive preference purchase choice to raise the sale effort to the brand of any products when consumers need to make purchase choice in time pressure consumption environment, e.g. seasonal discount sale period, products or foods shortage supply period, without any forever sale possibility in market. Hence , it seems that brand loyalty building factor will influence any brands of products /foods /service sale or provison number to be raised or reduced in possible. Also, it can explain why and how it has close cause and effect relationship between time pressure consumption environment and the brand loyalty building to the brand of products/foods/services to any marketers nowadays.

What are the in-store and out-store factors influence supermarket fast moving consumer decision

It is one interesting question: How can the brand of product seller influence the supermarket/store fast-moving consumers' more visual attention when the supermarket/store visitor is hurry to make decision to choose to buy which brand of product in time pressure environment? Supermarket/store fast-moving consumers do not usually spend much time to say in any supermarket shelf locations to choose numerous similar alternative brands of products. However, I assume the fast-moving supermarket/store consumer's decision is dependent on the interaction between the supermarket different shelf location sale environment and the mind of the consumer. So, the eye tracking explores this rapid processing that lacks conscious access or control to any supermarket or store consumers.

It brings this question: How product packing and placement (as in-store factors) and recognition, preferences, and choice task (as out-of-store factors) which will influence the supermarket / store consumer individual decision making process through visual attention. In split-second decision making, the ability to recognize and comprehend a brand of supermarket/ store product can significantly impact preferences. Hence, how the supermarket/store consumer's eye truly sees what whom mind is prepared to influence how much consumption desire to choose to buy the brand's product in short tim decision making process when he/she stays in the shelf location, it has less than ten or more than ten different kinds of brands products or foods to let the visitor to choose in the supermarket or store.

Brand owners and product developers will feel responsibilities to overcome promotion or advertising or communicaton challenge in order to let consumers to know their products are launched on the market. However, it is not until the product reaches the supermarket shelf that has good quality to the effort is judged whether it has how much sale number every day in the supermarket. The judges are the consumers themselves how to make decision quickly through the personal time pressure environment with minor package information processing in the supermarket.

What does it take to be consider an option to influence the consumers' minds on visual attention in point-of-purchase decision making ? The supermarket's in-store activities and the consumer personal out-of-store activities will influence how his / her visual attention to the brand of products in the supermarket / store any shelf locations when he/she is walking to pass any shelf locations. So, it seems that any supermarkets or stores brands of products sale number , it has relation to every supermarket or store visitors' visual attention throughout the point to point (shelf to shelf) decision making process in the supermarkets / stores. So, how much does the supermarket's visitors' time spending to obtain attention to the brand of produc? it will have possible to influence the brand of any products' sale number in the supermarket/store. Hence, in this limited timeframe, the consumer enters a decision making process that is in itself influenced by in-store and out-of-store both factors.

I shall explain what is supermarket / store space quality factor, e.g. top level versus floor level to different shelf variable height, weigh , or shelf space location factor as well as the product price elasticity and price-quality relationship to the brand of products both factors to influence every consumer decision making in supermarket/store. The in-store factor is more influential factor to compare out-of-store factor to influence consumers' decision in supermarket. For example, where the shampoo brand products are locating to be put on the shelf , it can influence the point to point behavior of shampoo product habitual buyers. If the buyer habitually chooses the shampoo brand products in the shelf location. Also, if all of the shampoo brand products are moved to another shelf locations to display its different kinds of shampoo products to cause the habitual buyer needs to spend much extra time to find where the another new shelf location is displaying the brand's shampoo products.

In this situation, information processing has a heightened decision making role as the buyer needs to spend much time to find where the brand's displayed shampoo products' shelf location to make non-habitual decision making between options. For habitual decisons, the consumer's visual attention is reduced to measuring visual search. However, when the brands of any shampoo products are moved to another new shelf location to display its different kinds of shampoo products. So, the act of another shelf new location search , it will influence the habitual shampoo buyer's visual attention to consider the brand of any shampoo products which are usually used to wash to his/her hair habitually. When he / she can find the other new brands of shampoo products are displayed on the old shelf displayed location of the brand of shampoo products. Hence, the traditional shelf displayed location to the brand of products, when the brand of products are moved to another new displayed shelf locations. This in-store factors that will influence traditional cosnumers through visual attention concerns to this brand of products more or less.

So, supermarket traditional shelf displayed variable location to the brand of products factor, which will have influence to the traditional consumers' visual attention to do either buying the brand's products or buying another brand's products to replace it, when the traditional consumer feels difficult that he/she needs to spend extra longer time to find whether where is the traditional useful product's displayed shelf location. Then, it will be possible to influence the traditional consumer's traditional purchase decision to the brand's product, and he/she will choose to buy another brand of product to replace when it can be displayed to the shelf location to attract the consumer's visual attention more.

It is one important in-store shelf displayed factor to influence the traditional fast-moving consumer individual purchase decision making behavioral change in any supermarkets or stores when they feel hurry to do personal time pressure consumption decision to make purchase final decision in the point to point counter purchase (the brand's of products are moved from the traditional shelf location visual attention moves to the strange shelf location visual attention) in supermarket time pressure consumption environment.

Hence, in supermarket time pressure consumption environment, in -store and out-of-sore both factors can influence fast-moving consumer individual purchase decision making. The in-store factors can influence product packaging, product placement components as well as the out-store factors can influence choice task, preference and brand recognition components. So, it is common to influence supermarket consumers choose do personal time pressure purchase consumption decision of visual attention purchase behaviors. The different brands' products are displayed to different shelf locations in order to cause shelf displaying products' different decision making effect.

However, instead of shelf displaying location factor, package will also influence consumers' decision making, due to the influence of minute differences in packaging design on visual attention. When, the supermarket consumer feels the brands are not familiar or unfamiliar. Then, he/she will spend more time to evaluate and verify the unfamiliar brands' products whether which one is value to buy in her/his decision making process. He/she will feel visual attention need in order to evaluate in set of brand alternatives to make conscious demand mind cognitive effort by involving working memory. So, if the product's package is attractive, even the consumer is unfamiliar the brand's any product choices which are displayed on the shelf location in the supermarket. The brand's attractive package factor can influence the consumer to raise whom visual attention. Then, the attractive package factor can increase much visual attention chance to many consumers when they are walking to pass through the unfamiliar brand's any products' shelf displaying location considerably. So, it explains when attractive package factor may solve the visual attention problem to fast-moving consumers when they are visiting one strange supermarket to find anywhere unfamiliar brand's products' shelf displaying locations. Because they are the non-traditional consumers to the unfamiliar brand's products, they won't be influenced to choose either buying or not buying the unfamiliar brand's products. When the unfamiliar brand's products are moved to another new shelf displayed location. So, if the unfamiliar brand has attractive package to let the non-traditional consumers feel visual attention when they are passing through the strange shelf displayed location. Then, it can raise purchase chance to the non-traditional consumers target number when they are staying in the strange supermarket. In conclusion, the brand of products' shelf displaying location and package factors may bring much influence to any traditonal or non-traditonal consumer behaviors in supermarket or store time pressure consumption environment.

What consumption is most
influenced in preference choice
by time pressure

What kinds of services or products are most influenced to consumer behavioral change by time pressure? Can time pressure factor influence more preference to other factors, such as age, culture, income level, habitual shopping, family or friend relationship etc. factors to influence consumer behavioral choice to these kinds of services or products in consumption market? I shall indicate some kinds of services or products consumption models to explain how time pressure can influence consumers to choose to consume its services or buy its products.

Firstly, for theme park entertainment industry example, has it time pressure to cause any theme park visitors, e.g. Walt Disney entertainment theme park to influence them to feel time pressure to enjoy their emotions to play any entertainment machine facilities and it brings negative emotion to choose the entertainment theme park entertainment consumption activities.

For Walt Disney entetainment theme park example, every visitor needs to pay a fixed ticket fee to enter Disney theme park. So, however, he/she chooses to play how many number of entertainment activities facilities, e.g. only one entertainment playing facility, or more than one entertainment playing facilities. The Disney visitor needs to pay the same ticket fee to enter Disney. So, it will cause th visitors feel unfair , they do not choose to play any entertainment facilities or play only less number of entertainment facilities. Because they need to pay the same ticket price to same to the visitors, who choose to play many entertainment facilities number in Disney. So, it brings this question: Does the Disney visitor feel time pressure when he/she chooses to play many number of entertainment facilities , but he/she will not enjoy to carry on other activities in Disney, e.g. shopping, visiting cinema to watch movies, walking around the whole Disney anywhere to view scene activities. Because US Disney entertainment theme park is very large . It has not only entertainment facilities to attract visitors to play. It has many places are value to visitors to visit or enjoy the other free charge entertainment activities , such as visiting Disney gardens, visiting ocean park, visiting Disney cinema to watch free movies, view scene or seeing free charge ocean animal performance shows , going to Disney shopping centres to shopping, visiting Disney library to read books, visiting Disney ocean park to view different kinds of beautiful fishes non-entertainment machine facility playing activities. All of these activities are value to any Disney visitors to choose to play or visit, instead of entertainment machine facilities activities. So, if one visitor hopes only to spend one day in US Walt Disney entertainment theme park. He/she will feel hurry to choose to play any machine entertainment facilities, or he/she won't choose any machine entertainment facilities to play in Disney because he/she also hopes to play other non-machine entertainment facilities activities, e.g. visiting garden, visiting ocean park, visiting library, visiting cinema to watch free movies, visiting garden to play free charge boats water entertainment activities, watching ocean animal show performance etc. different kinds of entertainment activities, even walking around anywhere fun and excite places in Disney theme park. Hence, the Disney visitor will feel time pressure to choose either playing any kinds of entertainment machine facilities or visiting different places in the whole one day in Disney.

Hence, time pressure factor may influence any one of Disney visitors how to choose any entertainment activities to spedn time in Disney. It will bring this question: Because the Disney ticket price is fixed fee, can the Disney visitor will feel unfair to cause negative emotion, if the Disney visitor feels time pressure to choose to play any kinds of machine entertainment activities or doing other non-machine entertainment activities in the Disney visitor's limited timeframe, during he/she stays in Disney? So, it seems that time pressure psychological factor will may influence some Disney visitors to feel unhappy, negative emotion, when they feel their entertainment activities choices are wrong or doing wring entertainment decision making in his/her limited timeframe. Consequently, time pressure factor will influence some feeling time pressure Disney visitors won't choose to enter Disney again. Hence, time pressure factor can have much influence to theme park visitors‘ behavioral change, instead of whether the entertainment theme park's machine entertainment facilities are attractive or enjoyable playing or how many entertainment facilities are supplied to let visitors to play in the entertainment theme park. So, entertainment theme park service providerd need to consider whether their ticket prices are reasonable to let visitors feel, if they do not want to reduce theme park visitors number seriously.

The another example is restaurant food service industry. Can time pressure influence food consumers to choose the restaurant to eat? Instead of food taste, price, seats available providing, restaurant location, public transportation facilities available etc. factors, which can influence the food consumer individual choice to the restaurant.

Is time pressure another one main factor to influence food consumers choice to the restaurant? In what suitation, food consumers will feel time pressure to influence whose preference restaurant choice? I assume that the restaurant 's price is reasonable, public transportation facility is convenient to catch to go to the restaurant, food taste is acceptable to the food consumer. Although all above these factors are accepted to the food consumer . But when the food consumer feels hurry to hope to find one restaurant to eat and he/she hopes to spend less time to sit down to eat in the restaurant , e.g. less than one hour. Then, the food consumer will compare all the restaurants are near to whose working place or school , if he/she is one student or one working person. Because he/she needs to eat lunch to go to school or go to office to work. So, the restaurant's food taste, price is not the main factor to influence him/her to choose to eat.

Otherwise, whether the restaurant needs him/her to spend how long queue time to wait, or/and the restaurant needs how long cooking time to let him/her to eat, the restaurant needs him/her to walk how long time to arrive the restaurant. All of these factors concern " efficient cooking time, queue waiting time serice performance" issues to the restaurant, which are the main evaluation requirements to influence the feeling time pressure food consumer to make decision whether he/she either still ought follow the better food taste, cheap food price factors to be preference decision or he/she ought follow short time queue time waiting or without queue time waiting, fast cooking waiting time factors to be preference restaurant consumption decision.

Hence, it seems that a feeling time pressure food consumer, he/she ought choose the restaurant to eat in preference when it does not need him/her to wait long queue time and wait long cooking time. Otherwise, when the food consumer does not feel hurry to eat, he/she outhgt choose the restaurant, it can provide good taste food, cheap price in preference to eat.

Hence, time pressure personal feeling will influence students or working people food consumers' preference restaurant choice when the restaurant can provide short time queue waiting or without queue waiting and fast cooking time service preference to satisfy their needs.

However , in some situation, time pressure can influence consumers to choose the service, even its price is expensive than other services. For example, public transportation tool choices service. When one passenger has need to find one kind public transportation tool to catch from the place to another destination, but the destination is far away from his/her location. He/she hopes to catch the kind of public transportation tool to arrive the destination about one hour. Although, his/her location has cheap public transportation tools to choose, e.g. bus, train, tram, ferry, underground train. But, he/she feels that all of these public transpotation tools need to spend longer time to compare taxi to arrive the destination. Although, these public transportation tools can be possible to arrive the destination withing one houe and they must charge cheaper fee to compare taxi. But, however the passenge hopes to arrive the destination in the shortest time. The most important influential factor is that the passenger feels personal time pressure to need to arrive the destination fastly and taxi public transportation tool is believed the fast transportation tool to arrive any destination to compare other general public transportation tools , when it has no traffic jam external environment factor influence. So, time pressure factor will influence passenger to choose taxi transportation tool in preference. Also, it seems that when the place often has many time pressure passengers are living. Then, the place's taxi business will be possible better than other locations. Hence, it implies that time pressure factor will bring need or demand number to be increased to some services.

Time pressure also influences how consumers choose to buy the kind of product, when he/she feels that the kind of product will be old fashin or it is not popular to use in society. For example, computer product, the traditional desktop large heavy weight computers will be possible to be replaced to use at home or office or any building places. Due to the laptop small light weight computers , it can be brought to anywhere by the users easily, even it can be brought to catch public transportation tool to use, it can be brought to restaurant, library, shopping centre etc. different public places to use conveniently. Due to some working people feel hurry to use computer to do their tasks, e.g. typing one document in short time. If they are not working in office and they have no computer on hand. They will worry about that they can not finish their tasks to give their bosses in limited time on the working day.

Hence, laptop computer will be one good chocie of task tool for busy working people when they need to often to use computer to finish urgent tasks in any time. Hence, it seems that the feeling time pressure working people will choose laptop computer in preference more than desktop traditional computer working tool. Due to the feeling time pressure workers, they feel that they can not finish their daily tasks in office. So, they will feel to need to use laptop computer task tool to help them to do office tasks . When they are catching transportation tool to go home or office time or lunch time , or holiday time. So, laptop computer product is more popular to time pressure working people target consumers.

Laptop computer products can also increase the feeling time pressure student consumers‘ needs. Because when one students feel home time is not enough to use computer to do their homeworkers at homes. When some students finish all lessons in schools and they need to catch public transportation tools to go home, in this catching public transportation time, they will be possible to hope to use one laptop computer to do their homeworks. So, one student who often feels time pressure to do whose homeworks, he will feel need to buy one laptop to carry it to anywhere, e.g. library, garden, school etc. different places. Then, he/she can do whom housework at any places in any time conveniently. Hence, it seems that their laptop computer products will be time pressure consumers' preference task tool.

In conclusion, the different factors influence consumer behaviors. Time pressure factor may be one main factor to influence consumers to choose to buy the kind of product or consume the kind of service in preference. So, when th consumer feels time presure to influence him/her to do preference choice to consume the kind of service of buy the kind of product. It is possible to occur to influence he/she does irrational economic choice decision. Hence, time pressure factor can being positive or negative both consumption emotion to some kinds of services or products . Hence, the increasing or decreasing number of consumers to some kinds of products or services, it has absolute relationship between of them. So, any product sellers or service providers can not neglect the importance of how time pressure factor influences consumer behavior in our nowadays society.

Time pressure impacts consumer
behavioral effect

I shall indicate cases to explain that how time pressure environment factor impacts consumer behavior as well as what effects will be brought by time pressure consumer behavioral cause. Instead of above discussions concern how customer personal time pressure psychological factor influence, whether hoe time pressure environment factor will also influence consumer behavior. What are the difference between time pressure environment factor and time pressure consumer personal psychological factor? I shall explain as below:

Firstly, the impact of life satisfaction is caused by time pressure on consumers responses. Can effective advertising can impact of life satisfaction when the consumer feels need to buy the kind of product in any time pressure environment? Can effective advertising bring direct impact on sales when the consumer feels need to buy the kind of product in time pressure environment? Effective advertising may being advantages, includes customers feel easy to accept of price increases, favorable publicity, and reshaping market segmentation.

However, when the customer feels need life satisfaction in time pressure lif environment. The time pressure life environment ought impact on the consumer responses on advertising. Hence, when the consumer needs to live in the time pressure life environment. The over-commercialization of advertising ought impact the consumer chooses to buy the brand of product, when the seller has attractive advertising to bring purchase incentives to influence consumption desire to the time pressure environment influential consumer. For example, when the summer season will change to winter season, the ice cream consumers begins to feel weather will change to cold weather. Because many people feel more colf in the beginning. This is seasonable time pressure environment feeling, it may influence many ice-cream likers feel ice-cream may be possible shortage in hot weather or summer season, due to many ice-creams will be bought in summer weather to cause supermarkets in possible. So, if the brand ice-cream can make attractive advertisement to persuade ice-incream number will be reduced in the coming winter season beginning. So, it may influence many ice-cream likers choose to buy this brand's ice-cream in preference in summer. Because they feel fear none of any this brand's ice-creams can be sold in supermarkets in summer. Because they feel this brand's ice-cream , it's problem to let they can buy any different kinds of ice-cream taste to eat from any supermarkets in summer season. Hence, it explains why effective or attractive advertising may increase sale number, when consumers feel the brand's product number will be shortage or reduced from the seasonal time pressure external environment factor influence.

Secondly, I shall discuss what is the relationship between the effects of product popularity and time pressure on consumer responses? When a brand is popular to let many customers to familiarize in society. Does it increase time pressure to influence consumers choose in preference? Time pressure remaining to product popularity concerns how much sale number is raised to persuade consumers to choose to buy a preference for ecommerce online shopping. It seems to be one time pressure online sale environment. The effects of the ecommerce online shopping environment has relationship beteen pressure and product popularity on perceived risk and purchase intention.

In ecommerce online sale environment time pressure is operationized at the time remaining for consumers to sign up the online seller' website and property popularity is operationlized to the number of products already sold at the moment when consumers visit the web page. Hence, when on online consumer has intention to buy any products from internet. He/she will attempt to type the product name, then he/she will find some webpages which can provide the different brands of product photos, their prices informations to let the consumer to compare whether which brand of product price is more reasonable, better quality , good product image from the web pages' advertisement information to let him/her to evaluate. Hence, any product web page will influence how every online custmer feeling is good or bad to the web page's any brands of products. If the consumer feel the web page has many high product popularity indicators, it may bring a high consumption desire to let the online cusomer to evaluate the web page all prodocts in order to compare which brand of product is the best to choose to buy in time webpage view pressure consumption environment. Otherwise, if the consumer feels the web page has high product popularity indicator , it may bring a less consumption desire to let the online consumer to evaluate any of the webpage products to choose to buy. So, online webpage advertising information will be one time pressure online ecommerce consumption environment.

I assume that online shopping consumers won't like to stay to view on any webpage long time. It is possible that they choose to click more web pages to hope to find more different familiar and unfamiliar both brands of products informations in order to make more accurate comparison and evaluation from more different kinds of brands of products in order to make the most accurate online shopping decision. Hence, any brands of products online webpage information will be one time pressure limited sale environment to consumers feel that they need to make the most accurate online purchase decision in short time. Moreover, it seems that if the brand of products which can be showed on the popular product webpage, the it will have much sale chance to let online purchasers familiarize in order to increase sale opportunity more easily.

Finally, I shall explain what is the meaning of external time pressure consumption environment is the long time queue waiting consumption environment. I shall explain how to achieve one simplistic queueing system to solve long time queue waiting problem to bring consumers' negative emotion influence to choose to consume the service or buy the product in preference.

For entertainment service example, e.g. queueing at the cinema counter to buy one ticket to watch the movie , or queueing at the music hall to buy one ticket to listen the music performance show activities. The audiences' ticket purchase aims to sit down in the cinema or music hall to enjoy to listen and see pretty music performance or watch the attractive movie comfortable within one to two hours entertainment time. If the movie or music performance show is attractive, the cinema or music hall will have many audiences accept to spend long time to queue to buy the ticket.

However, if the cinema ot music hall needs audience consumers to queue long time to buy the ticket, e.g. one houe , even more than one houe queueing time to wait to buy the ticket to watch the movie or listen the music performance show. Then, the long time queue waiting problem will be possible to cause a lot audiences number to be reduced, because they feel that they need to spend much time pressure to queue to by the ticket to listen the music performance show or watch the movie.

However, of these unacceptable too long queue time audiences can have another/ other cinema(s), music hall(s) to buy the same price , even more low price of movie ticket or music performance show ticket in short time. Then, they must leave the present cinema queue and go to the another cinema or music hall to buy ticket to watch the same movie or listen the same music performance show. So, long time queue is one external time pressure environment to influence consumer's preference choice to the service provider, when they feel it has another service provider does not need them or these audiences need to spend same long time queue time to wait to buy the ticket in order to enjoy the service, e.g. listening music performance show, watching movie.

Hence, in a high time pressure queue situation where decision makers, e.g. audiences have less time than needed (or perceived needed). It is very likely that they feel the queue waiting time stress of copying with themselves queue waiting time maximum limitation. So, if the movie ticket purchase audience feels that he/she will need to spend more than half hour to queue and half hour is himself/herself the maximum acceptable queue time level. So, his/her queue long time pressur negative emotion feeling will influence him/her to leave the cinema to choose another cinema. He/ she feels that ir does not need him/her to queue more than half hour in order to buy the ticket to watch the same movie in the another cinema, he/she can feel more comfortable to watch the movie. So, long time queue will influence some audiences choose aother service provider to replace it in possible short time, when they feel waiting in a queue is irritating, frustrating and hence costly.

What is a simplistic queueing system and how it can solve above queue problem. For a grocery store queueing counter case example, for one Apply brand computer shop example, the day's most busy queue time , there are about between fifty and hundred Apply brand potential computer buyers numbers every hour in the day. They need to queue to enquire the salespeople concern to any useful opinions to let them to know in order to make purchase decisions. But, the Apple brand computer shop lacks enough salespeople to answer their enquiries concern any computer purchase challenges. Every computer enquiry potential purchaser needs to spend at least half hour , even more time to queue to wait the salesperson to answer his/her enquiry in the counter queueing line. Hence, the feeling long time queue enquiry waiting consumers will feel time pressure to queue. Then, they will choose to leave the Apple brand computer shop's counter queue line. Consequently, the Apple brand computer will lose many potential computer buyers on the busy day.

The most simple solution is that it can increase the salespeople number in the most busy enquiry time every day. Hence, when every computer potential enquiry customer can contact every salesperson to listen whom opinion concerns his/her any computer enquiry issues in order to let he/she feels that they every one can provide excellent sale service computer issues enquiry explanation performance to satisfy his/her enquiry need to let himself/herself to feel in the short enquiry time. Due to they do not need to spend long queue time to wait every salesperson's feedback or opinion to solve their enquiries in the computer shop. Because they do not feel presure to spend long time to queue to wait the computer shops's every salesperson's opinion. So, they will raise satisfactory feeling to thie Apple computer shop's every salesperson individual sale enquiry service performance.

Consequently, the day's computer sale number will be possible to raise after the salespeople can spend much time to solve their enquiries effectively and efficiently.

● The reasons cause consumers feel time pressure

What factors can cause consumers feel time pressure to but the product in the personal time limited dominated consumption environment? It is one interesting question: Why does the consumer feel time pressure to make short time purchase decision making? I shall indicate some cases to explain this possibility as below:

First, I shall indicate household purchaser time pressure consumption behavior. Consumer house buyer behavior, some house buyer will feel personal time pressure to choose the different houses to make house purchase decision in short time. For example, if the house developer has a 30% discount house price to sell only in the short three months. So, after this three months, all house purchaser will need to pay the original house price. If the house developer's houses prices are between US doller one million to two million every house. For one million house price after 30% discount , the house buyer only needs to pay seventy million. For two million house price after 30 % discount, the house buyer only needs to pay one hundred and fourty million. So, expensive product's financing factor will influence the buyer's consumption time pressure, such as the house discount price case, due to the house developer's houses prices are very expensive. However, if any house buyers can make decisin to buy its houses in three months. Then, they can pay les 30% of the houses prices. Such as the original price one million house, the house buyer can pay less thirty million amount or the original price two million houses prices. The house buyer can pay less sixty million amount. So, the large discount financing amount may be attractive purchase method to influence many house buyers feel time pressure to decide whether they ought choose to buy the property developer's houses in these three months. It is one short term cheap house financing price to let many house buyers feel time pressure to make house purchase decision from this house developer in these three months . Hence, short term high discount price to expensive product financing factor will influence consumers feel it is right time to make pressure consumption decision.

Hence, such as this three months house discount price case, when the property buyer gain this property developer's knowledge of three months house discount price message. This sudden three months house discount price message will be one attractive knowledge of factor to impact the potential property buyers' house purchase desires to be raised in three months time pressure house purchase consumption environment. So, it is one feeling sudden time pressure consumption desire good example for this three monts large discount attractive houes price to influence house buyers to make house purchase decision from the house developer in these three months. Consequently, house developer will have possible to raise the large house sale number , if this 30 % house discount price can let many property buyers feel it is one worth purchase price in these three months. So, they will consider that they can not pay less 30% discount price to buy this house developer's any houses after three months. So they need to make house purchase decision in these three months short term time pressure house consumption market for this property developer.

So, this time pressure financing advantage will only bring benefit to this property developer, this time pressure financing advantage won't bring benefit to other property developers, because all property buyers feel need to make property purchase decision in these three months suddenly, due to this property developer can provide a special 30 discount price to any property final decision making to choose to buy its houses in these three months temporary short time. It seems that three months short time can cause final house purchase choice time pressure to any potential property buyers. They expect to gain high discount price to buy any expensive houses. So, these expenaive house potential buyers will feel need to make final expensive house purchase decision to choose to buy this property developer's expensive houses in these final three months perios. So, time pressure can occur in any short period, when the seller can provide any special sale promotion to persuade consumers to feel need to make sudden time pressure that purchase decision is they hope to earn special sale promotion consumption in the short limited sale perios for the seller.

Hence, consumer personal time pressure feeling, it can be predictive to any time occurrence pychological consumption, feeling, such as the property developer's sudden high per cent discount price to expensive house less dinancing burden factor to influence the expensive house buyers feel that whether they ought do choice house purchase decision in these short term three months , because the house developer's unpredictive and sudden attractive expensive houses reducing prices strategy. So, this property developer's short term three months high house discount price time pressure consumption strategy may persuade or attract , even encourage many potential expensive house buyers choose to spend lesser amount to buy this property developer's discount houses, either is paid by house mortgage bank loan lending payment method or installment payment method or on-time all payment method. So, the different house payment choice buyers will be influenced to make immediate property purchase decision in these three months time pressure period from this property developer's expensive discounted house number influence.

However, in this house market time pressure consumption environment, the property developer's expensive house supply number may also have influential effort to excite the expensive house buyers' house purchase consumption desires, for example, if the other expensive house property developers' between US one million and US two million of every property price's these houses in the country's property marker totel suppy number is one thousand property unit number. The potential property buyers , they plan to buy these amounts of expensive houses , the property needers estimate three thousand buyers number at least. Hence, it seems that these expensive house buyers' demand id more than three times to expensive property supply number.

Moreover, the other property developer's expensive property developers ' expensive house prices have no any discount in this three months periods, and some property developers' expensive house prices tend to increase 1 to 10 per cent in these three months period. Hence if the property developer can supply at least three thousand property units number between US one million and US two million sale price and all of these expensive houses are reduced 30 per cetnt discount to sell in these three months .

Consequently, it is possible to persuade all estimated three thousand expensive house potential buyers choose to buy this property developer's houses in these three months in possible. So, it explain that why this property developer's expensive discounted house supply number will influence these property buyers' preference choice. If this property developer has only one thousand expensive houses to be supplied by discounted 30% sale price. Then, it will cause shortage of expensive houses to satisfy these three thousand expensive house buyer estimated number in the country in three month discount sale promotion period.

Consequently, this property developer will lose two thousand these prices of expensive house potential buyers number in all these three months discounted sala period . I assume that all these three thousand expensive house property buyers will be influenced to make choice to buy its all dicounted expensive houses in these three month time pressure discounted sale period. So, it needs to do data gather concerns how many of thee expensive house potential house buyers number in its country in order to avoid discounted expensive houses supply number to cause shortage supply challenges and bring these expensive house potential buyers lose number in these three months period.

In conclusion, it explains why that supply number will influence this property developer's sale number in these three months sale period. Consequently, time pressure sale strategy ans supply number has close relationship to influence the seller's sale number in the time pressure sale period.

Secondly, I shall discuss how does environment time pressure factor influences consumer behavior? Does time pressure influence consumer donating behavior? I assume that external environment time pressure factor can influence consumer changes whom original purchase decision making. What circumstance's time can influence consumer individual to feel time pressure to consume. For example, when the consumer expects have one hour to choose whether which brand of product to buy among the different kinds of products. The circumstance is changed suddenly. It influences the consumers feel that they has only 10 minutes to make the final purchse decision.

Why does the consumer feel enough brand of product? What external circumstance factors influence he/she feels only 10 minutes time to make the final purchase decision suddenly? For travel fair time limited external environment influential pressure travelling consumption case example, the international travel fair can indicate that time limited pressure has positive significant influence on traveller perceived value and purchase intention in short time. In addition, perceived value is served as a mediating factor between the relationship of time limited pressure and feeling travelling entertainment purchase intention to the travel fair visitors. It has a beneficial reference for planning a travelling show or fair marketing strategy.

One attractive travelling fair/show can promote the country's different attractive travelling destinations to let the travellinf show's visitors to know. It can particularly influence the visitors' long time travelling planning , it can be shorten be short time travelling planning, e.g. after one year's travelling planning can be influenced to make immediate focused on choosing the country's travelling decision if he/she feels the country has more attractive travelling destinations, he/she prefers to go to travel in short time, e.g. within 6 months . So, when the travelling exhibition fair/ show can provide the country's beautiful scene photos to let the visitors to view. Then, it will bring effective time pressure feeling to let some travelling visitos feel travelling needs immediately in the travelling exhibition show/ fair . This travelling exhibition show/fair can bring the time limited pressure benefit. It is as an external environment factor that can influence the travelling visitors' travelling desires to be raised , when they can view many benefitical scene photos of the country' different undiscovered travelling destination . Then, it can increase their travelling desires to the country in possible.

I shall explain why travelling exhibition show/fair can play an important role in travelling consumer perceived quality and travelling country destination choice decision making to influence travelling visitors feel time limited pressure. However, perceived value has been show to be a value has been shown to be a value of perceived quality and perceived sacrifice to cause travelling visitors feel more interesting to choose to travel the country when they can view the attractive beautiful scence photos in the travelling exhibition show/fair.

A successful travelling exhibition show/fair can bring time limited process increases , the travelling visitors pay more attention to key travelling destination features and positive travelling information from the scene photos and travelling destinations introduction. So , the country's attractive travelling destinations scene photos and clear travelling introduction to different destinations information will be important message to let the different countries‘ travelling visitors to know when they spend a limited time to enter the travelling exhibition show/fair to view the different scene photos . If the travelling visitor feel very satisfied to the country's travelling exhibition show/fair. Then, this travelling exhibition excite whom travelling interest to choose to go to the country to travell in short time, when the travelling visitors are influenced to feel the country has many beautiful destinations where they feel have travelling interest in the limited time pressure travelling exhibition show/fair environment. If the travelling exhibition show/fair needs they to pay enter fee and it has only two hours or less time to premit to stay in the travelling exhibition show/fair.

Hence, if the time pressure limited travelling exhibition show/fair can let the travelling visitors feel attractive and enjoyable view feeling when they look every the country's any scene beautiful photos and indication how to the different travelling destinations and explains why the country's travelling places are value travelling destinations to let the exhibition visitors to know, when they do not know or discover these any one of value travelling places in the country before. Then, this limited time staying travelling exhibition show/fair will bring positive time pressure to influence some travelling visitors feel interesting to visit the country's inknown or undiscovery travelling destinations in short time. So, all attractive travelling exhibition shows/fairs are one external environment time limited positive pressure factor to excite some travelling visitors' travelling desires in short time in possible.

Instead of travelling exhibition show/fair can bring external environment positive limited time positive pressure to excite travelling visitors‘ travelling consumption desires, the another external environment positive limited time positive pressure case is that mobile coupons of limited mobile phone sale number or discount mobile phone call payment plan in short time case. How and why mobile coupons can excite any mobile consumption and/ or mobile phone call user choice to the mobile phone sale company or mobile phone call service provider.

An effective mobile plane useful limited time beneficial purchase strategy can encourage some mobile phone consumers to choose to use the brand mobile useful phone call service plan immedicately. if the mobile phone call service plan is attractive to the mobile phone call consumer . For example, dynamic discounts strategies are used by marketers to send scaraity message which lead to higher consumers' mobile phone purchase intention. An utility increasing discount straregy provides mobile phone call users with an increasing discount over time (e.g. 30% discount for in-store consumption for 30 minutes, after which the discount increases to 40 % , an utility discount strategy provides the same discounts for mobile phone call users over a specific promotional period (e.g. 40% discount from 9AM to 5 PM) phone call using time. An utility decreasing discount strategy offers mobile phone call users with a decreasing discount over time (e.g. 40% discount for in -store consumption for 10 minutes, after which the discount decreases to 30%).

However, these three different discount strategies for bargaining have different impacts on outcomes. However, they have same influences to lead mobile phone call users feel time pressure to do choose whether this mobile phone call using plan is suitable. If the mobile phone call user feels this mobile phone call using plan is suitable to use, then this mobil coupon promotion strategy can influence mobile phone user feels limited time pressure to persuade him/her to choose to use its mobile phone call service under different time limitation, quantity limitation and discount strategies on the mobile phone user's mobile phone call plan using intention.

Furthermore, I hypothesize that the brand of mobile phone quantity, limited scarcity message that gives a perception that the brand of any kinds of mobile phones are limited for purchase, it will have a positive impact on mobilt phone consumers' perceived value of mobile products, leading to a greater tendancy to make mobile phone purchase decision immediately. Hence, mobile coupon is one type of price-incentive promotion. In various price incentives, discount strategy is a mode of price negotiation between the mobile product conumer and the merchant, such as the mobile phone seller , mobile phone call user and mobile phone call service provider.

However, mobile coupons offer discount under a time constraint to induce perceived scarcity. Scarce commodities are more attractive than those with plenty inventory due to the speciality and uniqueness of the former perceived by the consumer. However, scarcity has both forms. They incluce quantity scaracity can let consumers feel need to buy the product in short time. Otherwise, due to stock shortage or low inventory to influence they can not brought the kind of product. Time scarcity means products are for sale only for a designated

May time dominate consumption
final purchase decision making

Whether can time limited pressure dominate consumer individual to make more rational purchase decision? Can the consumer make more rational decision , when he/she has enough time to make final purchase decision? I shall explain why and how the consumer can make more rational decision when he/she has enough time as well as I shall explain that without time pressure environment. It may dominate consumers to make more rational or more accurate decision making.

I assume that it is the final time limited pressure day to nee the consumer to spend more nervous do time final purchase decision among the different kinds of similar products choices, e.g. air conditions . If the consumer decides that the day is the final purchase decisin to choose to buy one air conditin among these different brands of similar air conditions in the super store. So, if on the that day, he/she can not make any final decisin to choose which brand of air condition to buy on that final consumption day in the super store when the super store visitor sees the final air condition consumption day advertisement in this year in this super store . Then, he/she won't buy any air condition again if he/she can not buy on that day in this super store.

The another time dominates immediate purchase behavior is that I assume that one common air condition can not be bought in short time later if all air condition consumers can not make decision to buy any air condition in this super store. So, his/her personal time limited pressure can dominate whose final or condition purchase decision in this super store on that day. If the store has many different brands of air conditions to lead him/her to spend long time to compare which is th best worth to buy in this super store. Then, it will let him/her to feel difficult to make the air condition final purchase decision in the store on that day. Otherwise, if the super store has less different brands of air conditions to need him/her to spend less time to compare which is the best worth to buy in the store. Then, he/she may make the final air conditin purchase decision making more easily on that day.

So, the final air condition purchase day of the super store, the super store's air condition final day's time can dominate the air condition buyer to make air condition purchase decision immediately. Due to he/she feels that all of these day brands air conditions can not bought from this super store after that day. So, he/she needs to make the air condition purchase decision making in this super store on that final air condition purchase day in this year. Because it is the final air condition purchase day in this super store of all sir conditions products. If he/she can not make the choice to buy any one brand of air condition in this store. Then, it is possible that he/she will lose this store's final cheap price air condition purchase benefits. However, if this super store has too many brands of air conditions need him/her to choose. It will cause him/her to spend more time to choose. Consequently, it will cause he/she feels difficult to compare which brand of air condition is the best and he / she does not choose to buy any one in this super store.

Hence, this super store ought have less number different brands of air conditions to let every air condition consumer to choose in order to let they can make final air condition purcahse decision on this air condition cheap price purchase final day. So, less different number brands of air conditions will dominate the consumers to spend less time to make purchase decision immediately and easily on that final sale day in this super store. Hence, it seems that the super store's final air conditions sold day time will dominate many air condition visitors to make purchase decision when they visit this super store in summer season on that day in this super store. Because all this super store's air condition consumers do not expect that they can not buy the best quality of air conditin in this super store final sold day , due to air condition stocks number shorten challenge is not supplied enough on that final cheap purchase day in this super store. Consequently, that time pressure will increase to influence them to make the final air condition purchase decision in the final sold day' s short time, before this super store closing time on that day. Their time pressure feeling comes from the super store 's air condition number shortage supply in possibility. It will dominate them to make the final air condition purchase decision in this super store in short time.

The anothe time dominates immediate purchase behavior case is that I assume that one common picture painter(actor), he finds one architect to help him to build one house. The architect only needs to folloe his house picture to build one house. The common picture painter tells him that he will give him building expenditure and building profit after he helps him to build the house profit after he helps him to build the house successfully. After six months, the architect made one decision, he did not demand the famous picture painter paid him for the building service fee. But, he needed him give the house picture to him to replace the building service fee. Because the picture painter feels that he didn't need to pay the building service fee to him to buy the architect's building service in these six months building time. Hence, he accepted his offer to give his common house picture to the architect for his reward.

I assume that this six months time dominate the architect to make the final building service fee decision either acceptance the common picture painter customer's building service fee or acceptance his common house picture replaces the building service fee. However, the architect believes that this common house picture can have higher selling price to compare his building service fee income. Consequently, I assume that his evaluation is right, this house picture selling price is more than three times to compare his past six months's building service income. So, it proved that his choice is right, because he could earn more than three times of his building service income after he decided to accept the common picture painter's this house picture to attempt to sell it in the picture auction market. It seems that this six months long house building time can dominate these both buyer and seller's purchase and selling behaviors, such as this picture painter and this architect. When the architect has this six months enough time to let the picture painter to change his building service offer decision from building service fee payment to his common house picture offer exchange. This architect can achieve his intention to let him to accept his free house picture sold product exchange offer more easily. Otherwise, if the architect can not need six months to build this house, he only needs three months or less time to build this house, then it is possible that the picture painter won't accept his this house picture offer to replace his building service fee easily. If he considers that whether his this house picture's selling price has possible to sell higher price to compare this building service fee for this house picture. He will choose to sell this house picture himself. Hence, due to the picture painter can not sell this house picture in this past six months. So, in this six months period, the house painter can not sell this house picture in picture auction market. This six months period can dominate his low market worth

selling feeling to this house picture as well as it can influence him to make this house picture exchange decision to replace his house service fee.
The picture painter will ask himself, ought the house picture painter need to wait how long time to sell this picture in auction market, because he does not know whether the architect needs how long time to build this house? So, this house building time can dominate the picture painter's acceptance of the architect's this free house picture product exchange offer, which is easier acceptance or difficult acceptance . In this six month' house building period between the architect service provider and the picture painter house buyer. Hence,the house building time can dominate the house building provider and the picture painter's house building buyer both's house picture free exchange purchase change behavioral choice between of them influentially.
The another time dominates consumption behavior case is that time rich or time poor factor, e.g. one fast food famous restaurant , its success is not only due to its fast food good taste factor, its restaurant location whether is close to the time poor people's offices, it is one main factor. Because this fast food famous restaurant only choose to build its restaurants to close to offices in any large cities in different countries. Hence, the franchisees need to pay expensive franchise loyalty income to buy its franchise in order to it can supply fast foods to the franchisees to sell, but they also need to pay expensive rent to this fast food franchiser, due to their fast food restaurant locations has been chose to locate in the main cities in different countries from the fast food famous restaurant's location decision. Hence, whether long or short time fast restaurant rent period to the franchisees , which can dominate the fast food restaurants's royalty and rent income. For example, if one fast food franchisee only sign one year contract to buy the fast food franchisor's loyalty to help it to sell its fast foods only one year, because it does not ensure how many fast food consumers will choose to buy these fast foods to eat, due to its price is decided by the fast food franchisor. If the cities have other fast food restaurants to let them to choose, they may find other fast food restaurants to replace it to eat fast foods very easily. If this fast good restaurant is not the most famous and it operates only short time. So, it can not earn more fast food franchisees' confidence to accept to pay long time rent to operate its fast food restaurants in cities and pay long time royalty fee to it. Otherwise, if the fast food restaurant had operated its restaurant for a long time period to raise its fast food loyalty's to let many different countries' fast food eaters to familiarize or

acknowledg its fast food brand in popular. So, long fast food opersation time can confirm that it has many fast food eaters, they prefer to choose to eat its fast foods. It can increase the franchisees' confidence to choose to rent its fast food restaurants and pay royalty to it in preference. Hence, the fast food franchisor's restaurant operation time whether it is long or short time, this franchisor's fast food restaurant operating time pressure factor will dominate the fast food franchisees' choices to decide to pay how long rent sand franchise royalty income to rent its restaurant to do the franchisee's fast food business in the cities locations in different countries. So, it seems that the fast food franchisor's business operation time can dominate the frahchisees' choice.

In special , in fast food industry, time rich and time poor consumers behavior will dominate their fast food choices. Time rich people feel they have enough or too much time when time poor people feel time is a major constraint in their daily life. The explansion of the fast food business, and the increase eatting of fast food are indicators of this trend. At the same time, shorter working hours increased wealth and less pressure on domestic rountines have opened up new segments of leisure consumption. But, " free time" in certain areas has not for many people, lead to an increases feeling of time richness.

So, it explains that why many fast food consumers who feel not enough time to work daily. They are time poor working people usually. So, instead of fast food taste factor influences consumer number. The people who feel time rich or poor, e.g. employmet rich or poor lunch time to the employee, it will dominate the employee chooses to go to fast food restaurant in preference. So, the fast food restaurant can supply rich time to let them to eat lunch in short time, if the employee has less time to eat lunch or more tasks need hime to do on that day afternoon. Hence, feeling time rich or poor to the people factor, which will dominate some consumers' choices to some kinds of businesses, such as fast food industry, or for public transportation tool choice case example, one time poor passenger feels need to go to the destination in short time. The time poor passenger will prefer to choose taxi in preference, then it is possible train or underground train, next it is tram, fainally, it is bus or ferry public transportion tool choices. Otherwise, for one time rich passenger, he has more time to go to the destinaton. The time rich passenger will prefer to choose the cheap public transportation tool , such as bus, ferry, underground train, ferry, train. The final choice is taxi. So, passenger's time pressure will influence whose public transportation tool choice.

● Time pressure dominiates consumer psychological factor

What are the factors of time pressure dominate consumer purchcase psychological behaviors? How any why do this time pressure psychological factors dominate consumer behaviors? It is possible that time pressure can dominate consumer mind and behavior either choose to buy the product/ consume the service or not buy the product/consume the service. Every consumer's final purchase decision, he/she is influenced how to make by himself/herself personal psychological limited time pressure . It means that he/she will have one time maximum standard to demand himself/herself to make the final purchase decision in whose individual psychological time standard (the consumer's individual psychological limited consumption time). So, it seems that ever consumer's final decision how he/she chooses to buy the product or consume the service, his/her consumption behavior will be dominated by whose psychological time limited consumption pressure.

So, time pressure issue seems evolutionary psychology, it looks at how consumer behavior has beed affected by psychological adjustments during time pressure evoluation. It seeks to identify which consumer psychological traits are evolved through adaptations, e.g. time pressure consumption adaptations to choose the final purchase decision in the final time limited consumption pressure environment, e.g. the consumer expects this day is the final day to choose to buy what kinds of the product. If he/she can't make final purchase decisin on the day, he/she will choose to buy the kind of product later, even he/she does not choose to buy the kind of product in the first or again, that is the products of natural selection, or the supermaket visitor case, he expects to choose which kind of food to eat within final 15 minutes, if he/she can't make the final decision to buy what kind of food to eat within final 15 minutes in this supermarket , or the restaurant eatting consumer case, he is queueing to wait to enter the restaurant to eat. He/ she expects the final queue waiting time is 15 minutes maximum. If after this 15 minutes, he/she can not be permited to enter this restaurant, then he/she will choose to leave this restaurant and he/she will find another restaurant to replace it. So, it seems that any consumer will have himself/ herself consumption limited stardard time to decide whether he/she ought choose to buy any products or consume any services in any consumption environment.

Hence, the cause of consumption time pressure dominates consumer behavior, it is based on these hypothesis: Every consumer has demand characteristic and time pressure can dominate how he/she make final decision to buy or not buy any product or consume any service as well as any consumer needs have time pressure consumption demand because he/she does not expect to epend more time to choose what kinds of products to buy or what kinds of services to consume. He/she expects to make purchase or consumption final decision in short time.

IN fact, consumers will be encoded to influence how they make final purchase decision. There are three main ways in which product information can be encoded. They include: Visual (product picture) ; for example, the conumer stores the memory by visualizing it as on product image. Aconstic (sound); here the consumer stores the information as a sound , this explains why some consumers sometimes get the brand name(words) that sound the same mixed up when they try to remember them. Semantic (meaning); here the object is stored in terms of what it means rather than as an image or sound, e.g. when the brand of toys can let many children feel fun to play. Then, when many parents feel familiar to the toy brand, they must remember this toy brand company is selling any kinds of toys to let children to play. So, famous brand can let consumers familiarize what products that it is selling. Such as the toy brand company can let parents feel its toys are fun to let their children to play. All these sensory information can dominate consumers make final choice purchase behavior to buy its product or consume its service in preference in any time limited pressure environment, if the brand can give positive information memory to let many customers to remember.

So, it seems that consumers are dominated to choose which kinds of products to buy or which kinds of services to consume by positive or negative emotion, time pressure in any consumption environment immediately. It is one time pressure consumption environment theory factor, it can influence consumer behavior is changed in any consumption environment time. Consequently, it explains that why time pressure can dominate consumer behaviors in possible. Also, any product seller or service provider needs to consider how to manage consumption time process to be longer to cause its consumers doe not choose to buy its product or consume its service consequently.

Methods avoid consumers
feel time pressure

In business society, it seems that any consumers will feel time pressure to cause their purchase decision making process changes in any consumption suitations, when they feel time pressure either by themselves or third parties influence, e.g. not buying any thing, not consuming any service, irrational making consumption final decision etc. consumption behaviors. How to reduce their time pressure to avoid they do above consumption behaviors. I shall indicate some consumption suitations to explain how to avoid their reducing consumption , due to time pressure factor influences as below:

Firstly, I shall indicate supermarket consumption environment example. In general, supermarket visitors will expect to spend less time to visit any supermarkets to make choice to biy any foods. They will stay short time when they expect to buy less foods, even, they will stay more short time when they expect to buy more less foods in any supermarkets. So, any supermarkets will need to calculate their clients' limited time pressure how to influence their foods consumption number. If the supermarket visitor expects to spend maximum 20 minutes to buy any foods in the supermarket. Then, he may choose some different kinds of foods to buy, e.g. icecream, fruit, bread, jam, fish etc. different kinds of foods, Otherwise, if the another supermarket visot expects to spend maximum 10 minutes to buy any foods in the supermarket. Then, he may choose less different kinds of foods to compare the first one, e.g. fish, jam, icecream only or bread, fruit , jam only. So, the second one supermarket visitor will buy less different kinds of foods, because he expects to spend 10 minutes maximum , his shopping spending time is less 10 minutes to compare the first one supermarket visitor. Because different supermarket visitor personal time pressure will limit him/her to choose more or less different kinds of foods to buy. However, time pressure will not influence every kind of foods number because every kind of food purchase number will not be influenced to buy more or less , due to the supermarket visitor personal time pressure variable factor influences his/her foods purchase number. Otherwise, the different kinds of food choice will be influenced to choose to either buy or not buy , due to every supermarket visitor personal time pressure is different.

Hence, supermarkets can focus on how to avoid any kinds of food purchase choice loses , due to supermarket consumer personal time pressure influences. In fact, in supermarket every shelf, it usually has many different brands of every kind of foods to let supermarket visitors to choose to buy. For example,the kind of jam food number has many brands are placed on shelf to let them to choose, e.g. there are more than 10 different brands of jam food are placed on one shelf. It will bring one choice problem. IF one supermarket visitor expects to choose one brand of jam within 5 minute, then he finds the shelf has more than 10 different brands of jam are placed on the shelf. Then he will feel time pressure to cause difficulty to choose the best brand of jam to buy from these 10 brands of jam. It will bring the negative emotion if he feels that all of these 10 brands of jam taste and price has no more difference. Consequently, these 10 brands of jam choice will cause he can not make the final jam purchase decision within this 5 minutes individual time limited. Anyway, if there are only 5 brands of jam are placed on this shelf, then the 5 minutes time limited consumer will has less brands of jam choices, it will influence him to do more easy choice to buy one kind of brand jam food from the shelf. It is one limited time pressure of psychological choice factor to influence any consumers feel to do any brand of food choice more easy in short time. Hence, I recommend supermarket shelf ought place every kind of food brand maximum to 5 brands , it is the best food brand number to every supermarket's shelves to let any consumers to choose different kinds of foods to make the easy food choice way in supermarket food market.

So, in super store market, it is similar to supermaket market. Super stores' main products are cloths, shoes, bags, stationarys, electronic products, e.g. fans, air conditions, televisons, radios, warmers, washing machines, dry machines, computers etc. However, super store visitors will like to spend more time to stay in any super stores, due to they feel to need more time to make purchase decision in order to make the most right choice to buy these any products. They usually expect to stay half hour , even one hour or more time in super stores. Their time pressures are depended on whether what kinds of products that they expect to buy in the super store. For example, if the super store visitor expects to buy one laptop computer. He will expect to make purchase choice decision within half hour, even more time. Otherwise, if the super store visitor expects to buy stationery, e.g. pen and rubber and pencil, he will expect to make purchase choice decision within 10 minutes. So, when the super store visitor expects to buy the product is more expensive, then his time pressure time will be longer than the super store visior expects to buy the product is cheap, such as stationery and laptop two kinds of products.

However , due to super store 's expensive and cheap product consumers whose time pressures are different. So, brands choice number will have much different between them. For laptop example, due to superstore visitors can accept to spend longer time to make laptop purchase choice. So, one shelf can place 5 to 10 different brands of laptops , another shelf can place 5 to 10 different brands of laptops to let them to choose. Otherwise, for stationery example, due to superstore visitors can not accept to spend longer time to make stationery purchase choice. so, one shelf can place less than 5 brands of pens, the another shelf can place less than 5 brands of pencils or another shelf can place less than 5 brands of rubbers , another shelf can place less than 5 brands of rulers to let them to make purchase choice in short time.

Secondly, for restaurant eaters example, when one restaurant has many eaters choose to enter this restaurant to eat its food, then it only chooses to let some eaters to enquire ticket number to queue to wait. Of course, some eaters will not like to wait too long time, so they will leave the queue to choose another restaurant to replace it in possible. For example, in afternoon eating time, these are two busy eaters, the student feels hurry to go to school or the working person feels hurry to go to office after lunch, although the restaurant service staff had given him one ticket to let them to queue to wait. However, their expected queue waiting time is within 15 maximum, but there are many eaters are queuing and their ticket numbers are small numbers. So, they feel that they must not enter this restaurant within 15 minutes themselves limited queue time. Consequently, their late entering this restaurant after 15 minutes issue will influence that they will choose another restaurant in possible. So, the restaurant long time queue will cause some eaters choose another restaurant in busy time. I recommend that the restaurant can limit every eater's eatting time, e.g. it calculate every eater's restaurant entering time and it limits every must leave the restaurant within half hour in busy eatting time. It can post notice to let them to know in the front door, e.g. Every eater needs to leave our restaurant within half hour, otherwise, you will need to bring your food to leave please. So, every eater know that they need to eat all food within half hour, otherwise, they need to bring their food to leave this restaurant. Then, this restaurant can increase more seats to let many queue waiting eaters , they do not queue to spend long time to wait to enter this restaurant. Consequently, many queue waiting eaters will choose to enter this restaurant, due to their queue waiting times are not exceed their time pressure limited time.

The final case is cinema queue . In general, any cinemas will have many audiences need to wait to buy tickets to watch movies. However, if the cinema has many audiences , they need to spend one hour, or two hours , even more than two hours to queue to wait to buy the ticket to watch any movies in the cinema. If some audiences' expected queue waiting times are within one hour. So, if these audiences' expected queue waiting timesa are more than one hour. Then, they will choose to leave this cinema and choose other cinemas to replace it in possible. How to avoid these time pressure audiences losing number increases in cinema busy time? I recommend that this cinema ought increase ticket purchase counter service staffs number , e.g. opening more three to five ticket purchase counters number in order to let these one hour time queue time waiting audiences can purchase ticket to watch their movies within one hour. So, opening urgent ticket purcahse service counters number issue is depended on whether there are how many audiences are waiting to buy ticket in the cinema in the time. However, it is only one best way to avoid the cinema audiences number loses in cinema busy time.

Time press how influences video playing game consumer purchase behavior

I shall explain that why it has relationship between the video game student consumer individual learning time and the working people individual working time both can influence video game playing consumer individual video game choice behavior. I shall assume that the different kinds of video game content difficult or easy win competition and entertainment spending on playing time factor will have more influence how the student or working person individual choice of what kind of video game purchase. Otherwisem evey video game price and brand and video game entertainment design content will have less inflience to every video game consumer individual purchase choice.

Why do the every video game's learning playing time and the playing time is spent to satisfy the feeling of winning game both factors will be the main factors to influcncc thc fccling busy lcarning studcnt or fccling rcst working personal target video game playing consumer individual kind of which video game software purchase choice? Why do feeling busy learning students or feeling rest working people will be prefer to choose to buy the kinds of need spending little time to learn to play to achieve the easy winning of the video game content aim in short time?

Nowadays, the different brands of video game products have different prices, various entertainment design contents and the easy or difficult win content feeling to be promoted to sell to satisfy the students or working people video game players' entertainment needs. However, time pressure will be one important factor to influence students of working peoples' video games choices. I shall explain that the time pressure factor how will influence the feeling busy learning or feeling rest working video game players or video game content software consumers to choose to buy the kinds of video games softwares which can let them to feel to spend little playing and learning time and they can feel easy to win the the video game competition in short time preference in this electronic enterainment video game industry.

Nowadays, video game target customers, they are young students and adult working people in common. When , the student does not need to go to school and he/she stays at home, he /she will like to play video game after he/she finishs to learn just a moment usually or the adult working person finishs jobs on the day, after he/she ate dinner, he/she will also like to play video game at home. So , video game can be one kind of entertainment product to let they feel enjoy to play when they re staying at homes.

Video game can be one kind of entetainment culture or entertainment behavior at home to them in popular. A player's ability to perform within a game entertainment is important, and players tend to knowledgeable about their achievements and failures within any game world. So, when one student hopes toget pass grade in school examination. He will choose to spend little time to attempt to win the video game content competition in short time because it can let him to feel that may increase his confidence to pass the grade in the school examination later in possible when he ensures that he had won the video game content competition. He believes that he can be trained to raise whose judgement and mind and analysis abilitiy in his playing visdo game proceed. Instead of playing video game can increase student learning confidence, it can also increase the working people's confidence, when the working person hopes to be promoted or increased salary later from his supervisor's appreciation. He will attempt to spend little time to win the kind of video game content competition in short time. He will have more condifent to achieve to raise his working performance to let his supervisor appreciation if he can learn how to win the kind of video game competition in short time.

It seems that whether the player needs to spend how much time to learn how to win any kind of video content game competitin , this " spending learning time of winning any video content game competition in time pressure playing environment feeling factor will influence the student or working person 's video game content purchase choice. If the video game design is more complex or difficult to let the player to feel to learn to win the game competition as well as it also needs them to spend more long time to learn to play and win the kind of video content game competition. Then, it has possible to influence the hard learning students or hard working people video game consumers, they do not choose to buy any kinds of need spending long learning and playing time to win the kinds of video content game competitive software products. So, it seems that the spend how much playing and learning time to win the video game content competition factor will bring time pressure to let the hard working people or hard learning student video game consumers choose to buy the video content game software products are easy to learn to play in preference because they expect to pass grade or appreciate easy, if they feel that they can learn how to win the video game content competition in short time as well as they do not spend much playing time to win the kind of video game content competition and they will reduce their learning time at homes.

I shall explain why price won't be the main factor to influence video game players' purchase choices in preference. Some video game software sellers feel reduced sale price can attract many video game buyers' choice in preference. It is one wrong mind, due to video game software price is not too much high, it is one kind popular cheap entertainment software product. So , the kinds of similar entertainment content design video game products , their sale price difference between the kind of most expensive , the highest price video game software and the kind of the cheapest , the lowest price video game software won't be difference very much. Their price difference level may be US 410 to US$50 or even less than US$50 level. So,, one video fame entertainment player won't feel that the kind of similar content design of video game software's higher price which will influence he chooses to buy another cheaper similar of kind video game content design software product to replace to the prior higher price one. Because their price difference are not too much or video game software entertainment product is not on kind of expensive product to let them to feel. So, it seems what video game software price won't influence the video game players' prior one of preference choice, it is not easy to be replaced from later cheaper one, when the video game player feels like to play the kind of high price of video game content software before.

Can the video game content influence player individual purchase motivation in preference? In fact, there are many different kinds of video game contents to let players to choose. This free-to -play busines model that has rapidly speed to achieve games services to general . So, some students or working people players can free download some kinds of video game softwares to play from online channel. It will be attractive to the no paid video game players. Hence, free download video game content will influence the paid video game players‘ purchase decisions for in -game content are not only affected by people's existing general attitudes, consumption values, and movitations , but also by the design decisions and the needs built into the game by the developers. Because the paid video game players won't like to buy the similar content video games, which can be free download to play from online or internet channel. They will feel infair or not worth or loss if they choose to pay to buy the similar video game content entertainment software, after they discovered that they may be free download this kind of similar video game content to play from internet.

It will bring this question: Why will time pressure influence video game player chooses to download free video game to play in preference? When one student feels that he has no enough time to study, he won't choose to fo to any video game shops to do video game software comparative behavior to compare which one's price is lower, game playing content is more attractive, brand is familar in order to make final purchase decision in preference. If he discovered that there has one kind of video game content, which can be free download to play from internet or online channel . So, when the student feels that he needs have much time to study on the day. Hw will choose to attempt to find some kind of video game contents from computer tool which has the attractive entertainment content , it can let he to feel enjoy to play and it is free download from mobile or computer. Then, he won't choose to spend unpredictive time to visit any video game shops to make purchase decision on that day. So, time pressure will be one factor to influence some video game software consumers to feel whether they ought either visit any video game shops to make purchase choice or download some free video game contents at homes for the feeling no enought learning time student players. Even time pressure will also influence adult working people video game players, when the working person feels tries after his full day busy working on that day. Then, he will want to stay at home to rest . Although, he expects to visit any video game shops to choose which video game software product(s) to buy on that day, but when he discovered taht there are some video game contents which ar attractive to influence him to do free download behavior from internet at home. Also, he feels very tried and he will choose to stay at home on that day. If he can find some free video game contents are attractve to influence he chooses to do free download video game contents behavior and replace visiting video game stores behavior on that day. So, free download video game content entertainment activity will be one attractive promotin video game software method to assist the video game sellers' new video game products to let many feeling time pressure learning or working video game players to know from internet channel.

Consequently, online free entertainment video game content download playing choice will influence many video game shops will lose many feeling time pressure video game players number every day in possible. Also, it means that the lazy students or disliking learning students or no job people or (less working hours) part time working people, they will be the main target video game customers, due to they accept to spend much time to visit their video game shops to choose any kinds of video game softwares to buy in preference.

● How can video game advertisement method influence feeling time pressure and feeling without time pressure video game software consumer purchase purchase?

In fact, video game sellers can choose new media chnnel to advestise their new video game software products, e.g. computer online advertisemen channel, instead of video game pictures in shops, magazine, newspapers, television, radio ,cinema, public transportation tools poster traditional advertisement channels. However, computer online advertisement channel can attract many feeling learning time pressure of students consumers and feeling lack of enough rest time working people consumers to let them to choose to view their video game software advertisements from online websites at homes conveniently.

It is easy to understand , due to these feeling lack of enough learning time student video game players and feeling lack enough rest time working people video game players, they go back home after they finished learning in schools or they finished jobs in workplaces on that video game purchase planning day. After they eat their dinners, they may turn on computers to search information from internet. Suddenly, they discover some attractive video game contents photos or images are advertised from the video game seller's website or public yahoo websie , even they can choose to buy any one of these video game softwares from online shopping channel. Then, they will feel convenient to buy any one of these video game softwares from internet channel. SO, online video game advertisement will be the feeling time pressure video game players' first time contact channel at homes or the fastest advertisement contact channel to compare visiting video game store post advertisement, television , radio , magazine contact advertisement channels, when they are staying at homes.

Due to internet is popular to be used to search any information for consumers. So, the traditional magazine, newspapers, television, radio and visiting video game stores advertisement channels won't be more attractive to the feeling time pressure video game consumers . They will chooce to find any information from internet at homes in preference , when they have at least one computer to use at home, they can click website to search any information from internet easily.

The most important factor is that they can feel to spend little time to search information from internet to compare spending more time to find anywhere places whether they has magazines or book stores to sell video game magazine and newspapers publishers, radios and television won't inform them when they have video game advertisements to let they know whether what new video game softwares will promote to sell as soon as possible when they buy newspapers or turn on radios or televisions at home.

Otherwise, internet will be easy to let the feeling presure video game software consumers to know when whose liking new video content game software(s) will be promoted to sell from internet advertisement easily. Also, the feeling time presure video software consumers can choose to buy their liking video game software (s) from online shopping channel in possible if the video game seller can provide one website to let him/her to pay visa to buy and then it can deliver the video game software(s) to his/her home immediately or tomorrow or later time when the buyer's home located in overseas or far away from the video game seller's warehouse and their softwares are needed to be delivered by air plane transportation.

So, the feeling time pressure video game players won't need to leave their homes to spend more time to visit any video game stores to make final video game purchase decision any time. Hence, online advertisement and shopping channel will be one good sale promotion method to any feeling time pressure video game players nowadays. It will influence the traditional visiting video game stores' video game consumers' purchase behaviors to change to online purchase behaviors at homes conveniently, because they avoid to waste much time to visit video game stores as well as avoid to waste much time to choose any video game products in different video game stores, when they are staying in different video game stores. Visiting video game purchase behavior will need they spend whole day time to make final purchase choice, even it is possible that they can not make any video game softwares purchase decision after they visit many video game stores on that day.

Otherwise , online game advertisment channel can let them to feel to spend little time to search any new video game contents from every web page as well as every web page can show the new video game content images or photos or pictures to let every online users to see clearly when he/she sits down to turn on computer to search any kinds of video game content information to view at home in short time.

In conclusion, online video game advertisement and online shopping channel can attract many feeling time pressure video game players' consideration when they need to search any kinds of new or old video game contents information and it also changes their purchase decision to online shopping from traditonal visiting video game store shopping behavior. Video game industry's advertisement method , sale method is the kind of video game playing content's easy or difficult feeling degree , spending how much playing time to win the competiton in the game entertainment environment factors will influence the feeling time pressure video game players' final purchase decision making choice behavior to any video game software publishers nowadays.

Long time pressure brings poor performance and customer negative emotion reason

It has one interest question concerns: May salespeople ought spend long time or short time to explain the product's advantages in order to persuade customers to choose to buy the product morc casily? I assume that consumers do not like to spend long time to listen any salespople to explain whether what advantages of the product has as well as they they will feel time pressure to listen any salespople explain what the product has different characteristics to compare other kinds of similar products. So, if the salespeople can spend little time to explain what the product's difference and characteristics to compare the kinds of similar products in order to let the customer feels understanding what the actual functions to product owns and what benefit it can attribute to let him to feel satisfactory when he uses the product. Then, the " less product function explanation " will achieve easily sale to cmpare " long time product function explanation". Because customers will feel time pressure when they need to spend long time to listen any salespoples' long time product function explanation in shop. I shall indicate two variable salespeople case to explain how and why they can cause extreme positive and negative emotion to their same potential vehicle customers in the shop as below:

In one car sale store, there are two salespeople, their sale skills are different. The first salesperson likes to spend long time to introduce any styles of vehicles' function to let every vehicle potential customer to know as well as he will also explain their feedbacks to let they understand their enquiries clearly. Because he believes that his vehicle potential customer will like him to introduce evey vehicle's strengths and weaknesses and unique functions to let he/she knows clearly.

He believes that he can increase any vehicle sale chance after every his potential customer can spend long time to listen his " long time product function introduction" and his plans to spend 30 minutes at least for his every time vehicle function introduction because he also believes that he can increase any styles of vehicles sale chance if his potential vehicle customers can accept to spend 30 minutes at least to listen his vehicle introduction in the car shop. He feels that his clients ought enjoy to listen his long time vehicle function introduction and they can be persuaded to buy any styls of vehicles more easily if they can attent to listen his vehicle function introduction in long time. SO, his sale skill focus on providing lot of vehicle knowledge to talk to any kinds of potential vehicle customers. They include any new styles of vehicles' relevant productive skills, characteristics , functions, strengths and weaknesses comparison to other similar styls of vehicles. He feels that they are his students and they enjoy to learn different new and old vehicles; engines comparison interestingly and they ought not feel time consumption pressure to listen his any long time vehicle function introduction talking.

Otherwise, the another vehicle salesperson does not spend long time to explain any new and old vehicle's function, characteristics and provide vehicle engine knowledge to let them to know. He feels " less time vehicle function introduction" sale skill will persuade any potential customers to choose to buy any styles of vehicles from him more easily. His sale skill focuses on following every kind of occupation to every potential customer's occupation background and making the suitable recommendation after his judgement what will be his/her preferable acceptance by his less time vehicle introduction. So, he believes that different occupation background of vehicle potential cusomer will have different vehicle driving need if he can know what kind of job he/she is doing. Then, he can follow his/her occupation need to give the persuasive and rational and reasonable recommendation concerns which kinds of styles vehicle(s) is (are) the most suitable vehicle product to let the client to drive. So, he won't spend long time to explain any styles of new and old vehicle engines and characteristics and function and compare their strengths and weaknesses to let them to know or understand clearly. He won't feel they are his students and he will not assume that they have interest to learn different styles kinds of vehicle engines knowledge.

I shall explain three kinds of different occupations vehicle potential customers how their occupations will influence their vehicle choices differently as below: As above these two vehicle salespeople. The prior one must provide not enquire what their occupations are. He must provide all new and old vehicle engine knowledge to let them to compare. Otherwise, the later one must engine what their occupations are. He must not provide all new and old vehicle engine knowledge to let them to compare, because he believes that there are not all potential vehicle customers like to compare any styles of new and old vehicle engines to make purchase choice, even purchase decision consequently.

For one engineer occupation vehicle potential customer (client) example, he will be one proficient analytical and engine calculation person. The later salesperson will provide actual data calculation evidences to let him to know. So, this engineer occupation vehicle potential client's sale chance which depends on whether how much actual engine data calculation evidences which can be provided to let him to know. Then, this potential vehicle client will follow this later vehicle salesperson his all actual engine data knowledge to attempt to calculate and judges and make subjective observsations and compares to analyze different similar styles of vehicles engine structures and characteristics as well as compares the advantages (strengths) and disadvantages (weaknesses) of these siilar styles of vehicle engines. Instead of the actual engine data knowledge provision, the later salesperson also needs to provide these data, e.g. how much oil or gas driving useful consumption expenditure for the similar styles of vehicles every driving mile, every similar styles of vehicle repair maintenance

expenditure etc. actual data information.
So, the later salesperson only need to concentrate on providing these actual vehicle engine dat and energy useful and the possible maintenance expenditures to different similar styles of vehicles. He aims to let his potential vehicle client can make quality and characteristics comparison to judge whether which kind of styles of vehicle has the most excellent peformance more easily, then he can persuade him to choose to buy any kind of styles of vehicles in his car shop more easily.
Next, for another nurse occupation potential vehicle buyer example, if the later vehicle salesperson only concentrates on providing any new and old vehicle actual engineering machines data to let the nurse occupation vehicle client to know. Then, she will feel he is wasting her time or she will reject to buy any styles of vehicles from his introduction more easily. Due to her occupation is nurse, she is not proficient to engine data calculaton. She has patient respect personalty. I think that the later salesperson ought consider how to speak warmth and sympathy to let the nurse vehicle potential customer to feel his considerable vehicle introduction that he does not need to consider whether he can persuade her to buy this style of vehicle only. He can let her to feel that he is a sympathy salesperson and he respects to explain any styles of vehicles to let her to know. So, he ought let her to enquire any questions that she feels doubt concerns any styles of vehicles and he needs to concentrate explaining any answers to let her to know respectly in his whole talking time. Then, his sale chance will be increase in possible , due to her sympathetic feeling is caused from his talking and she will feel that he does not only respect that whether he can sell any vehicle from her.
Finally, for the television director occupation vehicle client example, he likes to contact any new things or know any new news and he is one owning creative mind feeling personalty. So, the later salesperson only needs to concenrate on introducing any new styles vehicles or the vehicles which general people feel difficult to find in any vehicle sale shops.
Thus, it seems that spending long time hard to introduction and providing any styles of vehicles engines knowledge sale skill can not be the most influential factor to persuade any potential vehicle clients to choose to buy this vehicle shop's any styles of vehicles more easily. Otherwise, spending less time to judgement whether what the occupation of vehicle client is and following whom occupation background and analyzing sale skill will be the suitable sale skill to persuade the vehicle client feels need to make the fast

vehicle purchase desire in short time. Because different occupation working people will have different working mode or attitude as well as their working mode or attitude will influence their vehicle purchase mode or attitude from the vehicle saleperson's sale skill. So, the vehicle salespeople ought follow whom occupation mode to decide how to talk his/her vehicle sale introduction to let whose vehicle buyer to know or understand rationally. In conclusion, spending less time vehicle strategic sale introduction skill will be more suitable vehicle sale method to compare spend long time traditional providing vehicle engine data knowledge, function, characteristics , features comparison method. It seems that long time vehicle sale introduction method will let any vehicle potential clients to feel that the salesperson is wasting whose time to listen his/her talking in the vehicle shop.

Consequently, any product sale chance will be influenced by how the salesperson's sale skill, it does not consider whether how long time the sale salesperson spends to let the potential client to listen in the shop. Because it is usually that clients will feel time pressure when they need to spend long time to listen any salespeoples' talking about explaining the product in shop. It also means that they won't feel enjoy to spend long time to listen any salesperson's talking between them. So, long listening time will cause potential client feels time pressure and it will brings negative purchase emotion and they won't be persuaded to choose to buy the product by the long time talking salespeople more easily in the shop. Otherwise, speaking short talking and listening time will cause enjoyable feeling to the client and it can bring positive purchase emotion to potential client and the saleperson's talking behavior can encourage the potential client to choose to buy the kind of product more easily in the shop.

Printed by Libri Plureos GmbH in Hamburg,
Germany